MOOSE HUNTING

WARNING

Moose hunting presents certain risks. Anyone following the techniques outlined in this book does so at their own risk and must be aware of their own limits and the potential dangers before entering the forest. The author and publisher do not accept any liability when it comes to using the equipment and methods mentioned in this book. In no case can they be held responsible for accidents that may ensue.

Laws and regulations vary from one region to another. Always inform yourself on the laws and regulations that apply to your hunting zone.

First published in French in 2015 by Les Publications Modus Vivendi Inc.
under the title *Chasse à l'orignal*.
© Réal Langlois and Les Publications Modus Vivendi Inc., 2016

MODUS VIVENDI PUBLISHING
55 Jean-Talon Street West
Montreal, Quebec H2R 2W8
CANADA

modusvivendipublishing.com

Publisher: Marc G. Alain
Editorial director: Isabelle Jodoin
Content editor, researcher and copywriter: Nolwenn Gouezel
Translator: Kate Bernard
English copy editor: Maeve Haldane
Proofreader: Heather Martin
Graphic designer: Émilie Houle
Page layout: Vicky Masse-Chaput

ISBN: 978-1-77286-026-9 (PAPERBACK)

ISBN: 978-1-77286-027-6 (PDF)
ISBN: 978-1-77286-028-3 (EPUB)
ISBN: 978-1-77286-029-0 (KINDLE)

Legal deposit - Bibliothèque et Archives nationales du Québec, 2016
Legal deposit - Library and Archives Canada, 2016

We gratefully acknowledge the financial support of the Government of Canada through the Canada Book Fund (CBF) for our publishing activities.

Government of Quebec - Tax Credit for Book Publishing - Program administered by SODEC

Printed in Canada

RÉAL LANGLOIS

MOOSE HUNTING

Foreword by
Stéphan Lebeau
and Yves Laroche

THE
RACK
MAN

MODUS VIVENDI

FOREWORD

At the start of my career as a professional hockey player with the National Hockey League (NHL), I looked on in envy as hunters prepared for hunting season. With no time to devote to hunting at the time (I was much too busy with the NHL), I knew that I would start hunting the day I hung up my skates.

I met Réal Langlois long before he was dubbed "The Rack Man." He inspired me, both as a hunter and as a guide. As soon as the opportunity presented itself, I enrolled in one of his classes in preparation for my first moose hunting season. With passion to spare, Réal shared his knowledge of these great creatures with me. From the preparatory tasks to how to approach such an animal, I quickly learned that Réal's success was in great part due to his attention to even the smallest of details.

Shortly after my training with Réal, I crossed paths with my very first moose—an incredible feeling, let me tell you! But my inexperience meant I came home empty-handed. A year later, armed with Réal's indispensable advice, I harvested my first moose, and ever since, I've been putting into practice all the techniques this great hunter has taught me.

By picking up this book, it is now your turn to benefit from Réal Langlois, a man who has spent the better part of his existence studying and trying to understand the behaviour of moose. It is with much generosity that he shares his expertise, know-how and hunter's secrets. In this book, Réal delves into the topic of moose hunting, covering every aspect and making it an indispensable, one-of-a-kind hunting guide.

STÉPHAN LEBEAU
Retired NHL player

Paul Grenier, Pierre Guilbault, Eugène Labelle and Maryo Pépin are among the finest moose hunting experts in Quebec. But the progenitor of modern hunting techniques is, without a doubt, Réal Langlois. Aptly nicknamed "The Rack Man," Réal has been proving his expertise both in Quebec and in the Yukon for over 40 years now.

Since 1976, Réal has amassed quite the following when it comes to his knowledge of moose hunting. In 2003, he released his first DVD, *The Rack Man in the Yukon and the Art of Moose Hunting*, in which he shares his own hunting techniques and some of the most breathtaking landscapes.

On September 18, 2008, after several years of studying the behaviour of moose in some of the Yukon's most beautiful forests, Réal hunted a particularly imposing moose with a rack spanning an impressive 193 cm (76 in.) across. Standing only 2.5 m (8 ft.) away, Réal shot the moose with a bow, fulfilling one of his lifelong dreams. This amazing feat, officially recorded by Pope & Young with a score of 249, remains a world record.

Year after year, Réal hosts conferences that are both renowned and accessible. Hunters everywhere are constantly demanding that he write a book full of his "right" hunting techniques. Well here it is! In this book, Réal generously shares all his secrets so that you can go out there and hunt that trophy moose you've been coveting!

YVES LAROCHE
Radio host and hunting and fishing columnist

MY FIRST ENCOUNTERS WITH THE KING OF OUR FORESTS

My first experience hunting moose was in 1976, when I was 16. I was with my father, Joseph-Aimé, near Lac Chassignol in Abitibi-Témiscamingue. We were six hunters in all, every one of us armed with a rifle. I had a Remington 30-06 semi-automatic equipped with a telescope (which I still own to this day). The morning of our hunting trip, my father set me up in a small watchtower located by a beaver pond. The group's caller was Patrice Mercier from Mont-Brun, not too far from Amos in Abitibi-Témiscamingue.

That morning, Patrice was calling by the edge of the lake, close to the beaver pond. A few minutes after his first round of calls, we heard a male answer back and start to make his way towards us. The moose had to skirt around the pond to reach Patrice. I saw the tops of the trees rustle. My heart started beating at a thousand miles a minute. Suddenly, the moose was standing right in front of me. I shot my rifle. The 2 ½-year-old moose dropped dead on the spot. I had just killed my first moose! I was thrilled and so proud of myself. It was the start of a passion that would follow me my whole life. In that moment, a new dream took shape—that I would one day be able to call moose like Patrice Mercier.

Over the next two years, I hunted in Abitibi with my father's hunting group. Afterwards, I organized my own expeditions in the area, as well as in Témiscamingue and even in Newfoundland. And with every trip, I became a better hunter. I started seriously studying moose behaviour in 1990, in the heart of the Louise-Gosford controlled harvesting zone. Harvest statistics were high in this particular hunting zone located in the Eastern Townships. I was using a bow where most other hunters opted for rifles. This fabulous region served as the backdrop to my hunting lessons as I spent much time studying the behaviour of wild game.

My father, Joseph-Aimé Langlois

I regularly killed small moose, but I also managed to hunt larger bulls with antler spans of over 127 cm (50 in.). The biggest and most beautiful specimen I killed had a rack of 144 cm (57 in.). What a memory!

In the early '90s, during a hunting trip in the Louise-Gosford controlled harvesting zone, I saw 18 moose, 11 of which were males, over a 500-m (546-yard) span along the Canada–US border. A veritable hunter's paradise! One day, as I was checking on one of my salt blocks, I happened upon a moose that ran off as soon as he spotted me. Back then I hadn't yet mastered my calling techniques. I had watched some videos of Gisèle Benoît, a naturalist well known for her studies on the behaviour of moose in Quebec. To approach a moose, she would use antlers made of Styrofoam (polystyrene). The idea inspired me: I decided to raise my bow above my head and go off looking for the runaway moose, all while calling and positioning myself within shooting range. My tactic worked –I killed that moose using my bow. That experience gave me the idea to approach moose using pieces of wood.

Back then, I spent a lot of time in the forest outside bow-hunting season, studying and observing moose. I realized that each moose had a distinct register and vocal range, much like us humans. That's when I realized that there isn't just one sound for imitating a moose, there are many! A hunter must call out, even when his call doesn't quite sound right, because it might cause the moose to react, either by attracting the moose to him or facilitating the hunter's approach to the moose. I used to question my calls a lot: Was I calling often enough? Were my series of calls too short? Should I pause longer between calls? It was only after spending hours, entire days even, in the company of moose that I truly learned how to hunt. Think back to when hunters used to call out to female moose every 20 minutes. Every hunter did this–it was *the* hunting tactic believed by all to work. I came to realize that every hunter was wrong, myself included! It was also during this time that I realized it's better to hunt with both feet firmly planted on the ground, rather than high up in the air in a watchtower, and that the best strategy is to pursue a moose, grunting and imitating his behaviour rather than remain silent and immobile in one spot. Prior to these realizations, I had had successful hunting trips, but all of a sudden I was better than ever, bringing home bulls with increasingly bigger racks.

Throughout this book, I will attempt to convey to you, in detail, what I believe to be the "right" way to hunt moose.

RÉAL LANGLOIS

"It was only after spending hours, entire days even, in the company of moose that I truly learned how to hunt."

CONTENTS

"Everything I know,
I learned from
the moose."

INTRODUCTION

My first conference on moose hunting dates back to the early 2000s, and for over 15 years now I've been writing articles for various hunting magazines. Over the years, and thanks to a growing interest in my techniques, I've often thought of writing this book–of which this is definitely not the first draft! No other book on the market is quite as comprehensive as this one when it comes to the king of our forests. For months, I gathered numerous articles I had written and honed my writing skills (with a little help, of course!) and inserted advice here and there so that hunters everywhere would be able to bring that coveted moose trophy home.

In this book, I share some of my most successful hunting trips, but I also recount some of my less successful expeditions. I did this to help you better understand how my techniques evolved over time. For years, I travelled the country, watching, listening and studying the great creature that is the moose, hoping to decipher its behaviour. Inevitably, I began to question some of the hunting techniques that had been used for generations. To be honest, I didn't invent a thing–everything I know, I learned from the moose. Believe me when I say that you need to think like a moose if you want to get close enough to shoot one!

Whether you're a novice or an experienced hunter, I hope this book leads to unforgettable hunting experiences.

CHAPTER 1

THE KING OF OUR FORESTS

Every hunter should be knowledgeable of the game he covets. Here is everything you need to know about the king of our forests.

PHYSICAL CHARACTERISTICS OF THE MOOSE
(ALCES ALCES)

• An adult male with a full spread of antlers is the most imposing animal in North America and stands taller at the shoulder than a saddle horse or any of its deer cousins, like the elk, white-tailed deer, mule deer and caribou.

• Moose have robust bodies, with long, slim legs that end in cloven hooves sometimes measuring up to 18 cm (7 in.) long. Their shoulders are arched and muscled, giving their back a humped appearance. Their head is large, with a nose that extends in a long arch. Their ears are elongated and relatively large.

• Most moose have what's called a bell (a pendant of fur-covered skin) hanging from their throat. This bell can measure up to 30 cm in length.

• A moose's coat varies from dark brown, almost black, to reddish or greyish brown in colour, with grey or white leg markings.

• In late summer and fall, a mature bull carries an impressive rack of antlers usually extending between 120 and 150 cm (47 and 60 in.) from tip to tip. The antlers begin growing in April, reach their full span by August or September and fall off during the winter.

• A moose has poor eyesight but an incredible sense of smell and hearing.

IDENTIFYING THE AGE AND SEX OF A MOOSE

Here are a few tips to help determine the age and sex of a moose:

• Antlers are the only foolproof way of determining if a moose is an adult male. If antlers are not apparent, the animal may be an adult female or calf.

• Adult female moose, also known as cows, usually have a triangular patch of white extending from the base of the tail to the base of the vulva.

• Viewed from the side, a calf's head is shorter than that of an adult's more rectangular one. Calves have small, delicate muzzles compared to adults, who have prominent, bulbous muzzles.

Moose hunting is regulated according to the age and sex of the animal (see page 32). **WHEN IN DOUBT, DON'T SHOOT!**

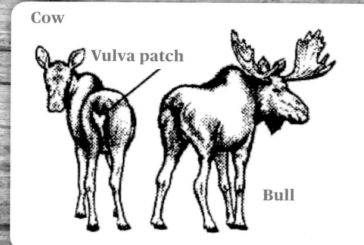

Cow

Vulva patch

Bull

Calf

Cow

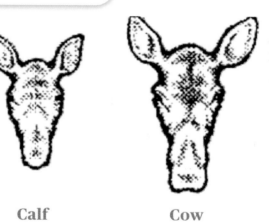

Calf

Cow

Source: Ministère des Forêts, de la Faune et des Parcs

HABITAT

Moose inhabit the great boreal forest (coniferous), as well as Canada's northern tundra and can also be found in mixed forests (coniferous and deciduous). Their range can vary between 10 km² (3.8 mi²) in summer and 2 km² (0.8 mi²) in winter.

During the summer, a moose's habitat must provide an abundance of lush leaves and mineral-rich foods. The most sought-after sources of food include the mountain maple, white birch, trembling aspen, willow, mountain ash and aquatic plants such as the lily pad. The lush forest cover is the ideal hiding spot for moose during hunting season. Moose do not tolerate high heat, which is why, on very hot days, they'll favour the dense forest over nutrient-rich open areas. Sometimes, they'll refuge themselves high up in the mountains, where the wind is stronger, or submerge themselves in water to help regulate their body temperature and escape pesky insects. When the leaves have fallen from the trees, moose seek out mixed forests, seeing as their fall and winter diet consists mainly of browse (i.e. twigs) and softwood. As winter progresses and snow begins to cover the ground, a moose's range diminishes and he tends to seek refuge in coniferous-dense areas.

A MOOSE'S DIET
Moose are herbivores. In the summer, an adult moose can eat up to 30 kg (66 lbs.) of vegetation daily, including branches, leaves, shrubs, upland plants and water plants.

BEHAVIOUR DURING RUT SEASON
Moose are polygamous. During mating or rut season, females cry out in an invitation for males to join them. Their cries can be heard from up to 3 km (1.8 mi.) away. Males answer with a grunt.

A FEW DIFFERENCES BETWEEN YUKON MOOSE AND MOOSE IN THE REST OF CANADA

	YUKON MOOSE	MOOSE IN THE REST OF CANADA
SCIENTIFIC NAME	*Alces alces gigas*. In the Yukon, you can also find the subspecies *Alces alces andersoni*.	*Alces alces americana*
SHOULDER HEIGHT	183 to 230 cm (6 ft. to 7 ft. 6 in.)	169 to 192 cm (5 ft. 6 in. to 6 ft. 3 in.)
TOTAL LENGTH	203 to 275 cm (6 ft. 8 in. to 9 ft.)	200 to 290 cm (6 ft. 6 in. to 9 ft. 6 in.)
WEIGHT	Male: 542 to 725 kg (1195 to 1598 lbs.) Female: 364 to 591 kg (802 to 1303 lbs.)	Male: 329 to 635 kg (725 to 1400 lbs.) Female: 227 to 408 kg (500 to 900 lbs.)
LIFESPAN	Up to 16 years in the forest	Up to 20 years in the forest (rare)
ESTIMATED POPULATION	Between 65,000 and 70,000	Approximately 125,000
AVERAGE DENSITY	1 to 2 for every 10 km² (3.86 mi²) Moose are concentrated in central and southern Yukon and inhabit only 15% of the territory. It's therefore common to have high densities in certain regions.	1 to 2 for every 10 km² (3,86 mi²)

CHAPTER 2

HUNTING LICENCES AND REGULATIONS

In Canada, hunting regulations are different for each province and sometimes even vary from region to region. This chapter mostly covers the regulations in Quebec and gives you information on what to expect when organizing a hunt. In most provinces, hunting can be practiced on private lands (make sure you have the owner's permission first) and public territory, also known as lands in the domain of the state. The three main hunting zones are ZECs (controlled harvesting zones, or Zone d'exploitation contrôlée), wildlife reserves and outfitter establishments. For information about other provinces, contact the ministries listed on page 221.

ZECs

Each province has their own hunting zone regulations. In Quebec, a controlled harvesting zone (ZEC or Zone d'exploitation contrôlée) is a hunting and fishing ground that is managed by a non-profit organization, and usually belongs to the state. To hunt there, you must register and abide by the dates, times and sites indicated in the registration document, and declare all of the game killed when leaving the territory. For more information, contact the organization that manages the ZEC you wish to visit.

www.reseauzec.com

WILDLIFE RESERVES

To hunt in a wildlife reserve in Quebec, you must make a reservation, obtain a right of access and abide by the dates, times and sites mentioned on it. Upon leaving the reserve, you are required to fill in a report and indicate the game killed.
www.sepaq.com

OUTFITTER ESTABLISHMENTS

Outfitter establishments are private enterprises that offer accommodation and services or equipment for recreational hunting activities. Some possess exclusive hunting rights, meaning you must obtain permission from the outfitter to hunt there.
www.canada-outfitters.com
www.pourvoiries.com

Uncharted territories

Do not hesitate to stray from territories already occupied by other hunters, for those hunters have likely been there for many generations. I suggest you take a hydroplane and head to a territory that can't be reached by road. If there are no roads leading to your hunting ground, you limit your chances of coming across other groups of hunters. The investment is well worth it, and believe me, there are still plenty of territories that have yet to be explored.

HUNTING LICENCES

To hunt, you need the right papers, and the laws vary from province to province. In Quebec, you need:

• A hunter's certificate;
• A hunting licence that corresponds to the type of hunting implement you intend to use.

To obtain a hunter's certificate in Quebec, you must:

• Be at least 12 years of age and have received the appropriate training for the hunting arm you intend to use;
• Have passed the requisite exams.

For more information on the training courses offered in your area, contact your provincial hunting and fishing agency.

Hunting licences are sold by sales agents and can usually be procured in sporting goods, hardware and convenience stores. You can also purchase them from certain outfitters, controlled harvesting zones and wildlife reserves.

A FEW IMPORTANT FACTS
ABOUT QUEBEC LICENCES

• A hunting licence must be signed by the person issuing it, as well as the licence holder themselves.

• A moose hunting licence, generally valid for a single hunting zone (see page 34), is also valid in all wildlife reserves, outfitter establishments with exclusive hunting rights and controlled harvesting zones where moose hunting is limited by quota. It's important to note that, in most hunting zones, restrictions apply concerning the use of a licence according to the date on which it was purchased.

• A hunting licence is personal and cannot be shared with another individual.

• Hunters must have their hunting licence on them at all times during an expedition.

• When a hunter kills game, they must remove the appropriate transportation coupon from their hunting licence and attach it to the animal.

Caution: Stay informed on your province's latest regulations.

For more information on hunting licences, contact your provincial wildlife agency (see list on page 221).

INITIATION LICENCE

An initiation licence applies to all Quebec residents aged 12 years or older who have never possessed a hunter's certificate. In such a case, the individual may obtain, for one year only, a special licence that allows them to purchase all the available hunting licences. In order to hunt, the individual must be accompanied by a Quebec resident aged 25 years or older who possesses the appropriate hunter's certificate. For more information, contact the Ministère des Forêts, de la Faune et des Parcs du Québec.

REGULATIONS

In order to preserve and protect our wildlife, hunting is highly regulated. All citizens who possess a hunting licence can practice hunting as long as they respect the regulations.

HUNTING SEASON

Moose hunting season varies by roughly a week across Canada and can vary even within a province. Mostly the season is from mid-September to late October, depending on the hunting zones targeted and the hunting arms used.

RESTRICTIONS DEPENDING ON SEX (MALE, FEMALE) AND AGE (CALF, ADULT)

In Quebec, only residents who possess a regular hunting licence can obtain a female moose hunting licence. Female moose hunting licences are awarded by random draw. Registration for the random draw begins in May and winners are announced mid-June. For more information, contact the Société des établissements de plein air du Québec (**sepaq.com**).

During periods when calf hunting is prohibited, only moose with antlers measuring 10 cm (4 in.) or more can be hunted. During periods when antlered deer hunting is permitted (and antlerless deer hunting is prohibited), hunters can also hunt moose with antlers measuring 10 cm (4 in.) or more.

BAG LIMITS

Bag limits are determined by zone, but generally consist of one moose per group of two to three hunters.

ARMS AND AMMUNITION

When hunting big game in Quebec, hunters must use one of the following arms:
- Rifles of a calibre equal to or greater than 6 mm: centre-fire cartridges;
- 10- or 12-gauge shotguns; single-shot cartridges;
- Muzzle-loading or breech-loading rifles and shotguns, without a casing, of a calibre equal to or greater than 12.7 mm, used with a single bullet;
- Bows with a torque of at least 18 kg (40 lbs.) within a draw of 0 to 71 cm (28 in.);
- Crossbows with a torque of at least 54 kg (120 lbs.) with a bowstring extension of at least 25 cm (10 in.) and equipped with a safety catch. The bolt must have a length of at least 40 cm (16 in.), including the tip;
- Arrows and bolts with a cutting diameter of at least 22 mm (⅞ in.).

Caution: Stay informed on your province's latest regulations.

HUNTING ZONES

Each province is divided into hunting zones. For example, Quebec is divided into 29 zones, each with its own set of regulations. Since zone 25 is reserved exclusively for fishing, that leaves a total of 28 hunting zones. Contact your provincial hunting agency for more information on hunting seasons according to game, bag limits and current regulations.

Moose population density varies from one hunting zone to the next (see page 61 for Quebec's chart on moose population density).

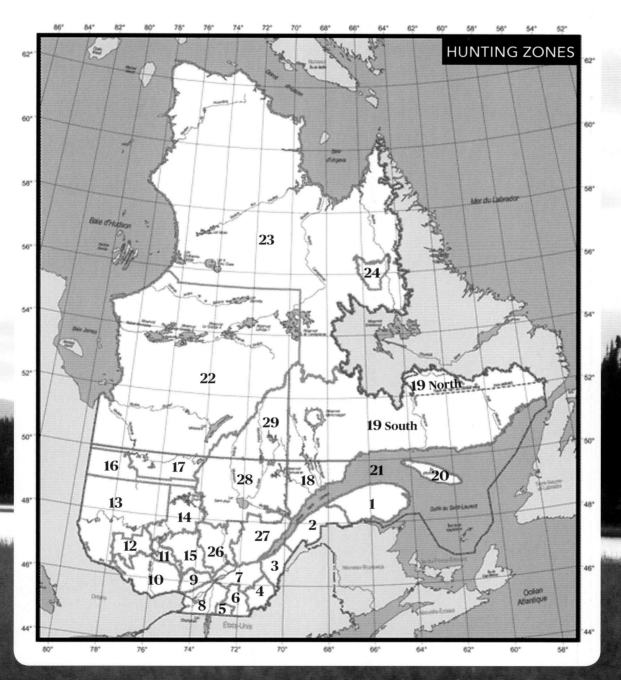

HUNTING ZONES

Source: Ministère des Forêts, de la Faune et des Parcs

THE NOTION OF A HUNTING EXPEDITION

It's important to define the notion of an expedition in order to determine who can attach their transportation coupon to the hunted game (see page 148). To hunt moose in Quebec, hunters must participate in an expedition. An expedition is defined as several people agreeing to team up with the goal of hunting together. For such an agreement to be considered an expedition in accordance with regulations, the involved hunters must share the preparatory tasks among themselves (planning, purchasing equipment, setting up the site, cooking, etc.) and see their project through (collectively entering the forest to hunt). In other words, the intention to hunt is not enough—all the hunters must be actively involved in the expedition.

A moose hunting expedition begins when the hunters agreeing to hunt together unite on a hunting site during authorized hours. All the hunters must be present and all must possess a valid moose hunting licence appropriate to the type of hunting implement used, hunting area and hunting period. Regulations stipulate that the expedition continues as long as one person in the group is hunting on the site on any given day. An expedition ends when a moose is killed or when all of the hunters in the expedition have ceased hunting. In the case of the latter, a new expedition must be formed before any hunting activity may be resumed.

Warning: Coming to an agreement after an animal is killed is considered an act of convenience, which is prohibited under Quebec hunting regulations. Take for example two hunters, both of whom have participated in the preparation of the expedition and procured the necessary permits with the firm intention of going hunting together. One of the hunters leaves town the evening before hunting season begins, while the second hunter arrives the very next morning. Upon waking, the first hunter is lucky enough to kill a moose, but because the second hunter was not yet on site when the moose was killed, a court of law could declare this an illegal hunt.

CHAPTER 3

HUNTING GEAR

Before heading off into the forest to explore, prepare your hunting grounds or hunt, it is essential that you arm yourself with the right equipment. Throughout the years, especially during my conferences, hunters have repeatedly asked me about moose hunting gear. Here is a detailed section on what I believe to be the basics.

ARMS AND AMMUNITION

Several different arms are authorized for hunting moose (for Quebec regulations, see page 32). Hunting periods vary by arm used, and some zones prohibit the use of certain arms. Implement regulations vary by province. Below are detailed descriptions of Quebec regulations.

RIFLES

According to regulations, hunters must use rifles of a calibre equal to or greater than 6 mm (.243) when hunting big game. Low recoil calibre (example: 308 win), standard calibre (example: 270 win, 30-06 sprg) and high calibre (7 mm rem. Mag., 300 win Mag, 300 Ultra Mag., 338) rifles are also permitted. I strongly recommend high calibre rifles because of the sheer size of a moose.

The lower the calibre, the higher the risk of injuring and losing the animal. For example, if you're 450 m (492 yards) away from your prey, you run the risk of missing your target if you're hunting with a 308. It's impossible to know ahead of time how close you'll manage to get to the moose, so it's better to always hunt with a high calibre rifle.

SHOTGUNS

I'm not a huge fan of shotguns as they have a too-short range in my opinion. When hunting with a shotgun, you must be in close proximity to your target in order to hit it.

BOWS

Today's bows are sophisticated hunting implements. Regardless of their features, the important thing is to know how to use them. There are several brands to choose from, such as Bear, Mathews and Hoth. For many years I've been using a Mathews bow. In fact, it was with this bow that I had the most amazing kill of my hunting career—I shot my prey from a record-breaking distance of only 2.5 m (8 ft.). What's tricky about using a bow is that before releasing your arrow, you need to be at most 30 m (100 ft.) from your target, which is not always a simple feat to accomplish.

CROSSBOWS

My crossbow of choice is an Excalibur, although there are other excellent choices, like the TenPoint. Hunting with a crossbow requires getting within 40 m (130 ft.) of your target.

Choosing the right hunting implement

For an easier hunt, opt for the long-range rifle, or if you think you'll be able to get in close proximity of your target, go with the shotgun. If, however, you're up for a bit of a challenge, try hunting with a bow or crossbow. Whatever hunting implement you choose, always make sure you're close enough to your target to kill it.

APPAREL

Thanks to today's modern technology, all serious hunters can equip themselves easily with apparel suited to the climatic conditions typical during moose hunting season.

Whether you hunt with a firearm, bow or crossbow, it's important that your clothes be as waterproof as possible, as silent as possible and as snag-free as possible (watch out for straps). Personally, I buy my hunting apparel and boots from Sportchief (**www.sportchief.com**). All their gear is waterproof, rugged, silent, odourless and comfortable, in addition to blending in perfectly with any hunting environment.

Opt for quality gloves. In cold weather, you'll be happy to have splurged on gloves that are just as well made as the rest of your attire. Too many hunters don't bother buying good-quality gloves.

I recommend the use of waterproof leather boots rather than the traditional rubber ones. I walk a lot when hunting and comfort is key. Make sure you break in your boots prior to wearing them hunting for the first time.

Here's a Rack Man secret: Bury your boots outside, cover them with dirt or mud and leave them there for at least two weeks. This way, they'll smell like nature. Personally, I find that rubber boots always keep their rubber smell and aren't very comfortable for walking for long periods of time on rugged terrain. However, if your hunting grounds are wet, you'll have no choice but to wear rubber boots.

SCENT CONTROL 101!

Regardless what make or brand of hunting apparel you choose to wear, the most important thing is to pay attention to your odour. When hunting, it's essential that you keep your natural scent to a minimum, which means that your clothes, undergarments, hats, gloves and boots must be as odourless as possible. Therefore, prior to making your way to your hunting grounds, it's important that you wash all your gear with fragrance-free detergent. Some hunters literally repel moose from their hunting grounds with their "human scent," which elicits suspicion in the animal. Don't forget that whether you're travelling by foot, all-terrain vehicle or motorboat, any unnatural scent may hinder your chances of harvesting a moose. The best thing to do is to regularly clean your gear (and yourself) with fragrance-free soap. You can find excellent hunting-specific products in most specialty shops. I strongly recommend washing yourself and your gear with fragrance-free soap even if you use effective scent elimination products (such as a scent killer) two to three times a day.

Furthermore, remember to be vigilant when storing your gear on your campsite. It's important to keep your gear away from any undesirable scents like cooking or gas fumes. Your best bet is to change your clothes the moment you enter your campsite and store your hunting gear in airtight plastic containers. And finally, avoid filling your all-terrain or motorboat vehicle with gas when wearing your hunting boots.

Camouflaging your odour is always a good thing when hunting, but sometimes it's not enough, especially when you're in close proximity to your prey. If when hunting moose you smell like a moose, your success is almost guaranteed. Specialty shops sell a variety of different scents. Personally, my "perfume" of choice is the urine of a rutting male. When I harvest a bull, I empty his bladder and keep some of his urine for next year's hunting season.

BACKPACKS

Choosing the right backpack, or shoulder bag, is important–you'll be wearing it every day, using it for exploring, scouting and hunting.

You're going to want a backpack that is comfortable, practical, quiet and waterproof. A camouflage pattern is ideal, but not necessary. Don't be shy about trying on several different models before deciding which one to buy–it's important that you find the one that's right for you. And then it's equally important to fill your backpack with the essentials. So what exactly are the essentials?

LARGE RESEALABLE BAGS (THINK ZIPLOC BAGS)

Fill one of your resealable bags with paper towels, which can be used as toilet paper or in lieu of flagging tape. Traditional red or orange flagging tape works fine during the day but can be hard to spot in the dark. Bonus: Paper towel is biodegradable, while flagging tape is not. Resealable bags also come in handy for storing the liver, heart or kidneys of any animal you harvest.

TWO FLASHLIGHTS: ONE HEADLAMP AND ONE SPARE

Make sure both flashlights run on the same battery type.

SPARE BATTERIES

It's best if all your devices require the same battery type.

A GPS
AND COMPASS

I prefer using a GPS that allows me to access topographic maps of the territory I'm hunting in. A compass is handy should your GPS break or lose its connection. Whatever device you opt for, make sure you know how to use it.

ROPE
AND TWINE

I suggest packing a roll of butcher's twine and some heavy-duty rope. Both will inevitably come in handy–whether for butchering, tying a bladder, etc. Believe me when I say, it's always convenient to have rope when you head into the forest . . . you never know when you might need it!

A ROLL
OF DUCT TAPE

Duct tape is sturdy and extremely practical–you can use it to tie branches or backpacks, make minor repairs and diminish friction noises. For example, if the pull tab on your brand new jacket makes noise, carefully wrap it in duct tape and, there you have it–silence!

TWO LARGE
ORANGE GARBAGE BAGS

These double as sleeping bags if ever you're forced to spend the night in the forest. Plus, they can help make you more visible to helicopter rescue squads should you get lost.

A SURVIVAL KIT

A good survival kit should be equipped with the basics: A whistle, hooks, some fishing line and matches. You can find some compact, yet comprehensive, survival kits in most specialty shops.

A FOLDING SAW

This kind of saw is very handy–it can be used to cut branches, carry out repairs and even butcher your kill. I don't pack axes or hatchets because over time they become much too heavy to lug around.

A KNIFE

I always carry a multi-purpose tool such as a Leatherman or Gerber in my back-pack. It's handy if I have any repairs to carry out or if I get into any kind of trouble. I also have my Victorinox 8-inch-blade butcher knife attached to my belt at all times.

BINOCULARS

I always bring my binoculars with me whenever I go hunting–they're a must for every hunter. Make sure yours are waterproof. For security reasons, it's important that you never use your rifle's scope as binoculars. I've been a fan of the Meopta brand for years now. Take your time choosing the right binoculars–you'll be using them your entire life!

A MOOSE CALL

I sometimes use a birch bark horn when I hunt. However, I prefer to call using only my hands and mouth. A horn is convenient when you want to call moose from a distance, or when you're dealing with strong winds. In such cases, your voice may not carry enough to be heard. A horn can be very useful for inexperienced hunters. Personally, I think it's always a good idea to bring a moose call with you, just in case you ever need it. Stores carry several different models to choose from.

WATER

Clean drinking water is essential–make sure to always pack a bottle or two in your knapsack.

OTHER INDISPENSABLE ITEMS

Before heading out, make sure to pack your cards, scent eliminator, rattling pallet, snacks (such as nuts) and your hunting licence and ammunition.

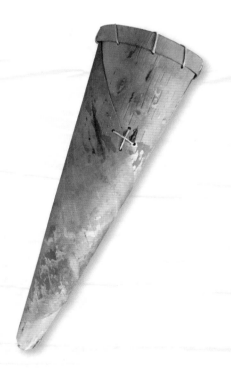

THE RACK MAN'S TOP PICKS

- Excalibur: Top-quality crossbows, made in Canada
  www.excaliburcrossbow.com

- Mathews Solocam: Bows
  www.mathewsinc.com

- Browning: Firearms
  www.browning.com

- Sportchief: Hunting gear and apparel
  www.sportchief.com

Inside The Rack Man's backpack

CHAPTER 4

WHERE TO HUNT

When it comes to hunting, the golden rule is simple: Go where there's game. Don't waste your time scouring areas devoid of moose. Instead, explore regions where moose density is high like wildlife reserves, outfitter establishments and, in Quebec, the ZECs. Inquire about the hunting success rates in such places. When it comes down to it, the most important thing is knowing where the moose are. You should also inquire about other hunters: Are there a lot of them, how many are there at any given time, etc. The fewer the hunters, the higher your chance of a successful hunt.

I always recommend doing a bit of preseason scouting in the areas you wish to hunt in. Remember, moose don't fly. They walk and leave tracks. If you spend an entire day roaming an area without coming across any sign that a moose has passed through (no broken branches, no half-nibbled leaves, no rut pits, etc.), stop wasting your time and move on to somewhere else. The more signs you spot confirming the presence of moose, the greater your chances of actually coming across one during your hunting expedition.

EVALUATING YOUR HUNTING GROUNDS

Eastern Quebec is home to the highest density of moose in the province. In Quebec's northern and western regions, moose are threatened by wolves (the moose's greatest predator), and their habitat is lower in quality compared to other regions, leading to lower reproduction rates.

Because of the high concentration of moose in Quebec, hunting success rates have increased considerably (20% between 2004 and 2010). In 2009, a record-breaking 27,000 moose were successfully harvested. This is in part due to the increase in moose population, as well as the increase in the number of active hunters. Between 2004 and 2010, there was a 17% increase in the number of licenced hunters. In 2009, more than 175,000 licences were handed out in Quebec alone.

MOOSE POPULATION DENSITY IN QUEBEC

HUNTING ZONE OCCUPIED BY MOOSE	AREA HABITAT (in km²)	DENSITY OF MOOSE/10 km² (approximations)	POURCENTAGE SUCCESSFUL OF HUNTS IN 2010
1	21,010	7.9 ± 0.9	21.6
2	11,649	6.8 ± 1.0	17.3
3	6,222	6.0 ± 0.5	11.8
4	6,392	1.7 ± 0.2	9.4
5	1,471	-	8.3
6	3,959	2.4 ± 0.4	8.1
7	3,904	2.7 ± 0.5	6.6
8	2,844	-	3.8
9	4,600	1.1 ± 0.2	4.2
10	18,767	2.4	5.4
11	4,190	1.4 ± 0.3	7.6
12	14,653	2.8 ± 0.3	8.2
13	52,300	3.1 ± 0.6	8.3
14	21,000	1.8 ± 0.3	9.5
15	11,879	1.8 ± 0.3	5.7
16	18,026	1.7 ± 0.3	11
17	20,170	0.8 ± 0.1	11.9
18	25,228	1.3 ± 0.2	9.2
19 SOUTH	149,100	0.4 ±	14.8
22	204,142	0.3 ±	24.6
26	16,999	2.3 ± 0.5	11.1
27	18,524	3.2 ± 0.5	17.2
28	60,724	0.9 ± 0.2	9.1
29	39,075	0.4 ±	18.4

Source: Ministère des Forêts, de la Faune et des Parcs

READING AN ECO-FOREST MAP

An eco-forest map gives an overview of a province's forest stands. It provides detailed information on a region's vegetation (forest type, density, stand height, age class, etc.), land type (bog, gravel quarry, etc.), hydrography (lakes, bodies of water, swamps, etc.), logging roads, topography, etc.

Eco-forest maps were designed by forest experts and are not easy to decipher at first glance. However, by attentively reading the map's legend, you can discover some useful information. You can purchase paper versions of these maps or download electronic versions compatible with your GPS. For more information on eco-forest maps of the areas you hunt in, contact your province's wildlife agency (see list on page 221). For Quebec, contact the Ministère des Forêts, de la Faune et des Parcs. (**www.mffp.gouv.qc.ca**).

An eco-forest map can be a very useful hunting tool, especially when it comes to understanding an area's vegetation. With an eco-forest map, you can accurately recognize and determine what territories are home to moose. I have to keep in mind which trees are in the area where I'll be hunting. Early in the season, moose have access to a wealth of food. Deciduous stands are widespread and I stick to the areas where they are most abundant. On the other hand, areas rich in conifers (example: fir trees and pines) are not as visited by moose at this time of year.

In the fall, you should stick to the areas where the moose go to feed. Look for regions that are rich in hardwood. In late September, I tend to gravitate towards hillsides and vegetation bordering burn areas. I seek out logging sites that are three or four years old with forage growth of approximately 1 m (3 ft.)–these are great hunting spots in late September and early October.

When the leaves start to fall, try seeking out areas with trees that lose their leaves later in the season. Throughout the years I've noticed that in some regions birch trees lose their leaves a little later, so stick to such areas, as moose love birch leaves. At this time of year, you should also look for areas rich in alders, trembling aspen, beech trees and other low-to-the-ground trees, seeing as the earth is already frozen over and devoid of leaves.

The dividing line between coniferous and deciduous trees is also a significant point of reference; I've noticed time and again that females visit such areas during rut season.

A FINAL PIECE OF ADVICE

Don't hesitate to download the Google Earth app as it provides aerial views of the land, which can be very practical during hunting season. www.google.com/earth/

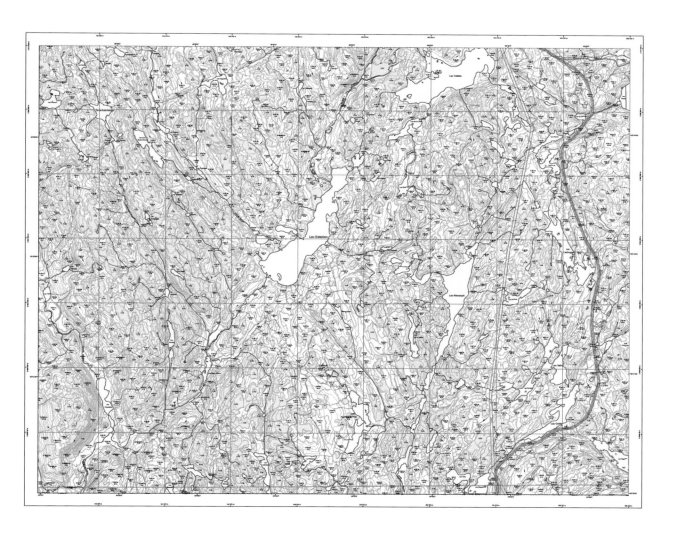

Source: Ministère des Forêts, de la Faune et des Parcs

TYPES OF COVER CROPS AND SPECIES ACCORDING TO THE INVENTORY PROGRAM

CONIFEROUS
Stands where 75% of the total surface area is covered by coniferous species.
R

DECIDUOUS
Stands where 75% of the total surface area is covered by deciduous species.
F

MIXED
Stands where coniferous and deciduous species each account for more than 25% but less than 75% of the total surface area.
M

CODE	CONIFEROUS SPECIES 3*	CODE	DECIDUOUS SPECIES 3*
G	White spruce	BB	Paper birch
E	Red and black spruce	BJ	Yellow birch
PB	White pine	CH	Red oak
PR	Red pine	EQ	Red maple
ME	Grey pine	ER	Sugar maple
PU	Tamarack	FT	Tolerant hardwood
R	Eastern hemlock	FI	Intolerant hardwood
S	Unknown conifer	FH	Humid hardwood
C	Balsam fir	FNC	Non-commercial hardwood
G	White cedar	PE	Poplar
		FI	Intolerant hardwood

CODE	CONIFEROUS SPECIES 4*	CODE	DECIDUOUS SPECIES 4*	CODE	DECIDUOUS SPECIES 4*
EB	White spruce	BP	Paper birch	FX	Unknown deciduous
EP	Red and black spruce	BJ	Yellow birch	FNC	Non-commercial hardwood
PB	White pine	CF	Shagbark hickory	FA	White ash
PR	Red pine	CC	Bitternut hickory	HG	American beech
PG	Grey pine	CT	Black Cherry	OR	American elm
ME	Tamarack	CM	Bur oak	PD	Largetooth aspen
PU	Eastern hemlock	CM	Swamp white oak	PA	Balsam poplar
RX	Unknown conifer	CR	Red oak	PT	Trembling aspen
SB	Balsam fir	EO	Red maple	TA	Basswood
TQ	White cedar	ES	Sugar maple		

1) Hickory, Oak, Ash, Beech, Walnut, Ironwood, Basswood (applies to 4th)
2) Ex: Poplar, Birch, associated Red Maple (applies to 4th)
3) Black Beech, American Elm, Rock Elm, Red Elm (applies to 4th)

DENSITY-HEIGHT INDEX							
AVERAGE HEIGHT OF DOMINANT AND CO-DOMINANT TREES							
	22 m +	17 m to 22 m	12 m to 17 m	7 m to 12 m	4 m to 7 m	2 m to 4 m	2 m +
Height class	1	2	3	4	5	6	7
Density class							
81% to 100% A	A1	A2	A1	A4	A5	SD	SD
61% to 80% B	B1	B2	B3	B4	B5	SD	SD
41% to 60% C	C1	C2	C3	C4	C5	SD	SD
25% to 40% D	D1	D2	D3	D4	D5	SD	SD
H	High coverage density						H7*
I	Low coverage density						I7*

*Information gathered via satellite image

AGE CLASS						
EVEN-AGED STANDS	10 (0 to 20)	30 (21 to 40)	50 (41 to 60)	70 (61 to 80)	80 (81 to 100)	90 (101 +)
UNEVEN-AGED STANDS OR MULTI-STORIED STANDS	Young uneven-aged or irregular stands (origin < 80 years)					
	Old uneven-aged or irregular stands (origin > 80 years)					
MULTI-STORIED STANDS	10-30	30-10	30-30	-	50-50	-	70-70	-	90-90	-	120-120	-

MULTI-STORIED STANDS												
	10-30	30-10	30-30	-	50-50	-	70-70	-	90-90	-	120-120	-
	10-50	50-10	30-50	50-30	50-70	70-50	70-90	90-70	90-120	120-90	-	-
	10-70	70-10	30-70	70-30	50-90	90-50	70-120	120-70	-	-	-	-
	10-80	90-10	30-80	80-30	50-120	120-50	-	-	-	-	-	-
	10-120	120-10	30-120	120-30	-	-	-	-	-	-	-	-

Source: Ministère des Forêts, de la Faune et des Parcs

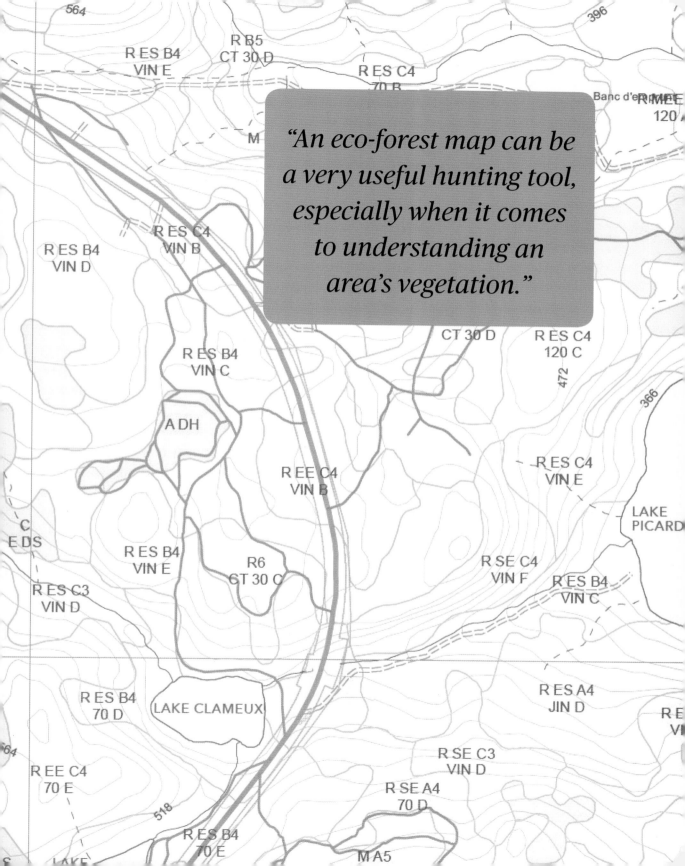

"An eco-forest map can be a very useful hunting tool, especially when it comes to understanding an area's vegetation."

UNDERSTANDING MOOSE MOVEMENTS

Throughout the '80s and '90s, I spent a lot of time in the Louise-Gosford controlled harvesting zone near Lac-Mégantic, as well as in the Yukon. It was during these formative years that I began to understand the behaviour of moose. As funny as it sounds, I'm still learning a little more each year, especially when it comes to moose movements.

Most hunters harbour stereotypes when it comes to moose movements. Of course, we all like to think we have a firm understanding of the patterns and travels of moose during hunting season. Renowned biologists have done studies on the daily, monthly and seasonal movements of moose across Canada and the United States. These studies are complex, extensive and, to be honest, hard to understand for us mere mortals! I myself have analyzed a few of these studies and can confirm that moose movements vary greatly from one region to another.

Studies show that seasonal movements are influenced by several factors, including food and water abundance, landscape, weather, species density and the presence of predators. Hunting pressure is an important factor to consider. In one region, it's possible that moose remain mainly within the same core area, while in another region, depending on the factors mentioned above, the core area may vary from season to season. With such varying results, it's not worth spending too much time discussing the relevance of these studies.

Studies on daily movements during hunting season also have fluctuating results. Generally, however, males tend to travel more than females during hunting season, while young males seem to cover more ground than the older bulls. The most influential factor when it comes to male moose movements in the fall would be the density in a given area. The more moose there are in an area, the less the moose will travel and vice versa.

FINDING THE BEST SPOTS

Don't hunt in vain! In other words, you can call as much as you want, but if there are no moose in the area you're calling, you'll never get a response! Prior to choosing a hunting ground, it's essential that you determine whether or not moose are present in the area. Be on the lookout for telltale signs–hoof prints, flattened grass where a moose may have lain, rubs or rut pits. If, after exploring an area, you haven't found any signs that a moose has passed through, move on to another area.

Generally speaking, moose return to the same areas year after year. At the end of your hunting season, make a habit of covering your territory by foot and entering all relevant information in your GPS. If you're lucky enough to be able to hunt deer and moose on the same land, continue searching for signs of your game in order to establish a basic approach to next year's hunting expedition. For example, establish where the breeding sites are by locating the rut pits.

If you're unable to properly explore your land in the fall, you'll need to head out in early spring, as soon as the snow has melted. The best time to prepare your trails and cut branches in order to access certain spots is at the end of the hunting season, before it begins to snow. I highly recommend preparing your trails outside of hunting season to avoid disturbing your game. Don't hesitate to identify strategic spots with flagging tape. By doing so, you'll be able to easily find your spots the following year.

RUT PITS

Rut pits are always a good indication that bulls are roaming the area and that you should hunt in the vicinity. I've noticed that bulls don't urinate in all rut pits, so it's important to find one that has been urinated in and exploit it. A filled rut pit suggests that bulls are nearby and is one of the most reliable signs that you're in moose territory! When you find a rut pit that's been urinated in (and believe me, you'll know if you have–the smell is unmistakable), it's like winning the jackpot! I recommend picking up some of the urine-soaked dirt and using it to mask your natural scent. When navigating the forest, always have a Ziploc-style bag handy–it'll allow you to collect and carry dirt from rut pits.

The scent of success

I can't say it enough: When you're out exploring your hunting grounds, it is absolutely essential that you mask your natural scent. By rubbing urine-soaked dirt (the most effective odour eliminator out there) onto your clothes and skin, you'll disguise your natural scent, allowing you to approach or attract a moose, who might even mistake you for one of his own (see chapter on rut pits, page 151).

MOOSE TRACKS

There are many opinions on how to read moose tracks. Perhaps you've been told that a female's hooves are more pointed than a male's, but believe me, no one can say with certainty simply by looking at tracks if the moose in question is a male or a female. I challenge anyone to differentiate the tracks of a 6 ½- or 7 ½-year-old female from those of a 3 ½- or 4 ½-year-old male. A moose's hoof size is directly proportional to the size of its legs and weight. What I can tell you is that, in general, large tracks usually belong to bulls.

When you come across moose tracks, the first thing you need to do is determine whether they're fresh or not. To do so, consider the weather. For example, if it rained that very morning and the tracks are still filled with water, chances are you're looking at fresh tracks. On the other hand, if you're dealing with a very hot day, the dirt will have dried quickly.

THRASHING

In early September, when a solitary bull begins to shed the velvet tissue covering his antlers, he begins to display unusual behaviour in the hopes of attracting a female. This unusual behaviour is brought on by hormonal changes. A bull will mark his territory by thrashing his antlers against shrubs and trees. If you come across several rub spots in one area, chances are you're in a bull's territory.

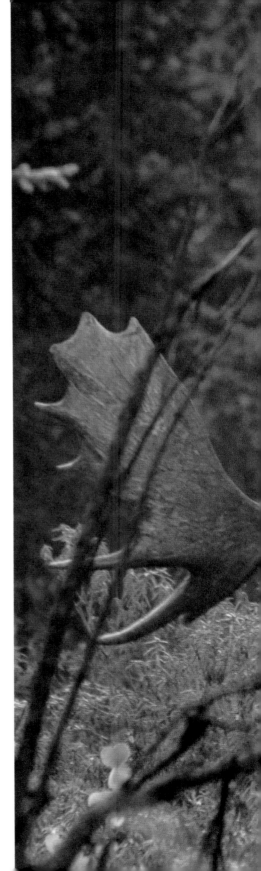

MOOSE SCRAPES

Moose sometimes scrape a 50-cm (20-in.) groove into the ground with their hooves–a visual sign that they consider that area to be theirs and theirs alone. These scrapes basically just serve to mark a moose's territory and are almost entirely odourless (and are not to be confused with rut pits).

I once witnessed a male scrape the ground and urinate simply to warn me that I was not welcome in his territory. By behaving like he did, he was letting me know that the area was his and that he was unhappy with my being there. And yet he was perfectly aware of the fact that I wasn't a fellow moose; I was standing 15 m (50 ft.) away, looking straight at him. Of course, his strange behaviour wasn't in any way part of his mating ritual . . . at least I hope not!

A large specimen in action; a bull can produce up to 50 scrapes during rut season.

FLATTENED GRASS

Moose are solitary animals, but they do sometimes lie in herds. When you're out scouting an area, keep your eyes peeled for large areas of flattened or mussed-up grass, as this could indicate an area recently occupied by one or several moose.

Before settling down in the grass, a moose will walk upwind and then retrace his steps in a sweeping arc. This allows the moose to catch a warning scent from any potential predators. Experienced hunters know when they should cease following a moose's trail and head upwind instead, in the hopes of catching their prey off guard.

CHAPTER 5

SALT LICKS: THE ART OF PREPARING YOUR HUNTING GROUNDS

Installing a salt lick is an excellent way of increasing your chances of harvesting a moose during hunting season. A salt lick attracts moose to specific areas by providing them with an abundance of mineral salts. By installing a salt lick in a given area, you'll attract a lot of the moose that happen to be nearby.

THE RIGHT PLACE AT THE RIGHT TIME

I find it shocking when hunters insist that salt licks are a complete waste of time, saying that they cost a lot and yield few results. I find this to be a strange way of thinking, considering the thousands of hunters who have successfully killed moose by baiting them with salt licks. Personally, I don't consider salt licks to be a hunting technique per se, but rather an efficient way of attracting as many moose as possible to a given area.

Just like all members of the deer family, moose naturally seek out mineral deposits after enduring the long winter months. At the start of summer, their need for mineral salts is especially strong: Females need them because they are lactating and males, because their antlers are growing. In the fall, the need for salt diminishes, but this doesn't mean they are any less attracted to it. However, it's still important to install your salt licks in areas frequently visited by moose.

As a general rule, cows visit salt licks more frequently than bulls. However, knowing that bulls answer the calls of females in rut, be proactive and install a salt lick anyway. To determine the best place to install your salt lick, you must keep in mind the areas visited by moose in the fall, not in the summer. Because salt leads to thirst, it's also a good idea to install a salt lick close to a body of water. Yet another good reason to do some scouting in between seasons.

I'm often asked during my conferences if it's important to prepare salt licks, and my answer is always the same: It depends on the size of your hunting ground and the number of hunters present. For example, the hunting grounds in the Yukon are immense, and your chances of running into a fellow hunter are extremely low. In such cases, it's not absolutely necessary to attract the moose to you–you can go to them. Not to mention that current Yukon hunting regulations prohibit the use of salt licks (check your province's regulations regarding salt licks). If salt licks were legal in the Yukon, I might install some, but with the unique goal of drawing as many moose as possible to one area in order to increase my chances of a kill. The smaller your hunting territory is, the more important salt licks are. If your hunting grounds are vast and include lakes and swamps, both of which provide an abundance of mineral-rich nutrients, you don't necessarily need to install salt licks. A large area allows hunters to move around in order to locate moose, while smaller areas limit a hunter's mobility, oftentimes forcing him to hunt exclusively from hunting blinds or stands for fear of scaring the moose off and into another hunter's territory. Having said this, I recommend installing at least one salt lick for every 160 to 200 hectares (395 to 494 acres).

The smaller your hunting territory is, the more important salt licks are.

SALT LICKS

One really important piece of advice when it comes to salt licks is this: If you decide to make one, make sure it's a good one! When it comes to moose, you're going to need lots and lots of salt. I've watched moose hunting videos where the natural salt licks cover more than 2 km^2 (0.8 mi^2). Now that's quite the salt block!

I own 90 hectares (222 acres) of land on which I built a 275-m^2 (329-yd^2) salt lick. Each year, I install four or five salt blocks (red or white). Depending on where you hunt, you could also use blue salt blocks. I have to stress that I've never had any success using blue salt blocks on my land, but I know for a fact that they are very effective in other regions.

THE DIFFERENT TYPES OF SALT BLOCKS

WHITE BLOCKS: Natural salt blocks

RED BLOCKS: Iodized salt blocks

BLUE BLOCKS: Salt, iodine and cobalt blocks

RED-BROWN BLOCKS: Mineral blocks
(salt, iodine, iron, copper, manganese, zinc or cobalt)

All my blocks are mounted on posts 1 m (3 ft.) high so that the moose can easily access them. Moose have really long legs, so having to crouch down to get to food on the ground is both inconvenient and uncomfortable. Moose have a natural tendency to go for food that is higher up.

PREPARING YOUR SALT LICKS

1. Find the biggest tree possible and cut it down to chest height. Trim its branches.

2. Using a saw, cut out a deep bowl-like hole in the trunk. Fill the hole with salt (three 20-kg [44-lbs.] bags should be sufficient). Don't hesitate to sprinkle salt around your stump. If you're dealing with hardwood, I recommend literally filling the hole to the brim with salt, in addition to mixing in 5 to 10 kg (11 to 22 lbs.) of minerals.

3. Place four or five salt blocks within a 5-m (15-ft.) radius of your stumps. Install the blocks on trucks that are at chest height.

MAINTAINING YOUR SALT LICKS

Every spring, as soon as the snow has melted, I add salt and minerals to my salt lick in addition to 10 kg (22 lbs.) of sulphur (the smell attracts moose), which I buy at a hunting store. I spread the sulphur on the ground, in close proximity to my salt lick. I top off my salt lick in late July or early August by adding about half the quantity of salt and minerals used in the spring.

CHAPTER 6

MOOSE TRACKING

When you step foot inside that forest, remember that you're entering moose territory. As a hunter, it's essential that you mask your natural scent and presence. Many hunters pay little attention to their scent, and even more neglect to prepare their clothes before heading out (see page 49). A classic example: A lot of hunters stop to fill their car with gas while wearing their hunting boots, or hang their clothes out to dry at their campsite right next to where they're cooking bacon or onions. Of course, regardless of whether you practice Stand or Spot-and-Stalk hunting, it's difficult to entirely eliminate your natural scent, but you can diminish it. Plus, there are products available on the market that are extremely effective at masking or eliminating odours. One last tip: Don't set up camp too close to your hunting grounds as your odour will betray your presence, warning off moose only dozens of metres away.

STAND VS. SPOT-AND-STALK HUNTING

For a successful hunt, I highly recommend stepping down from your stand and exploring the area on foot. Unless you're in an extremely small area, or one with an exceptionally high density of moose, Spot-and-Stalk hunting will increase your chances of a harvest. Stalk hunting doesn't imply pursuing your target like a wolf, but rather navigating the forest like a moose: Calling out, rattling against branches and without covering the sound of your footsteps. By remaining on the ground, you'll be able to slowly approach your target. Plus, you'll be able to practice your rattling technique, which is pretty much impossible from a tree stand. And finally Stalk hunting means your calls will sound like they're coming from the ground, not from up above, and calls from the ground sound much more realistic in my opinion.

Another advantage of Stalk hunting (and one I consider to be the ultimate secret to success) is that it allows you to cover your entire hunting ground and figure out where the moose hang out. The probability that a moose happens to be within earshot of a call when you're Stand hunting is relatively slim. Plus, during rut season (September and October), moose gather in particular areas, leaving large areas of the forest deserted. By practicing Stalk hunting and sweeping your territory, you have a much higher chance of spotting a moose than if you stand motionless in a blind. When you're Stalk hunting, you're more likely to suddenly hear the echoes of an answer to your call, or spot a family of moose as you're rounding a corner. With Stalk hunting, every step you take is potentially bringing you one step closer to a kill.

Of course, in a region where the moose population is high, Stand hunting can also be very effective. However, in my opinion, it's more advantageous and easier to find moose if you're constantly on the move. I suggest navigating the forest trails, all the while imitating moose vocalizations and noises.

WEATHER CONDITIONS

In my experience, when the weather is hot, moose tend to head to the mountaintops and keep their activity to a minimum. In such cases, the best thing to do is to follow them up the mountains, rather than wait for them to come down. It's important to note that even during rut season, if the weather is warm, they'll remain relatively inactive during the day, preferring to wait until nightfall to head out in search of food and females.

On calm, windless days, Stalk hunting is the best way to go, which means sweeping your territory on foot. If you try to advance in silence, a moose will think you're a predator. It's best to advance gradually, all the while calling and rattling. Both these techniques will be explained in detail in the upcoming chapters.

On particularly windy days, calling is not necessarily the best thing to do, but neither is staying at camp. On rainy or windy days, moose have difficulty distinguishing the noises they hear in the forest. There's a good chance your calls won't be heard, especially if you're calling from your blind. You're better off heading out in search of your target; head into the forest, scout and practice still-hunting.

Be discreet in your movements and don't call out. The wind and rain will cover any noise you happen to make, allowing you to sneak up on your target without startling it.

When the weather is mixed and the wind comes and goes, the most important thing is to control your natural scent. The best strategy on days like this is to stand guard near moose sites or salt licks. Remember to make enough noise so that the moose will hear you when the wind dies down. When moving around, make sure to walk upwind. When I navigate the forest, I always verify in what direction the wind is blowing, and my main objective is to locate and identify any sounds I hear. As soon as I hear something, I determine which path is the best and move in the direction the sound is coming from, staying upwind as much as possible. If moving upwind isn't possible, I try my best to avoid being exposed. Sometimes, approaching a moose with the wind at your back is unavoidable, which is why it's so important to always take great care to mask your natural scent as much as possible. To do so, make sure you always wash your hunting apparel with fragrance-free detergent and get into the habit of using odour eliminator.

NAVIGATING THE FOREST

One of the common hunting mistakes made by beginners is to try to make as little noise as possible upon entering the forest. Why is this technique so often applied? Simply because it's been the most widely taught hunting method for many years now. But I'm here to tell you to stop doing it. Moose weigh between 300 and 725 kg (661 and 1598 lbs.). That's big–in fact it's huge! With such an imposing frame, moose inevitably make a lot of noise when walking. Even if you're not a good caller, by navigating the forest while imitating the noises made by moose, you'll be more successful than if you move about quietly. Be careful–I'm not saying you should charge ahead like a bulldozer, just that you should mimic the sounds a moose makes.

When the ground is dry or frozen, you'll inevitable make noise when you walk. When this happens, remember to adopt the behaviour and attitude of a moose. This method may seem pretty basic, but believe me, it's very effective.

STRATEGIC HUNTING SPOTS

When choosing a hunting spot, the first thing I do is locate the "home" of a group of moose, keeping an eye out for any sign they've passed through (signs of browsing, rub spots on trees, rut pits, tracks, etc.). Such information not only confirms a moose's presence, but also gives me a pretty good idea of the kind of specimen I might find in a given area. For example, by measuring the dimension and length of antler rubs on a tree, I can determine if a large, mature bull is somewhere nearby.

I always walk and call, frequently stopping to see if I get an answer. When I do get an answer, I try to find a cleared, unobstructed spot where I'll be able to see the moose approach. It's important to ensure that you have at least three clear shooting lanes to where you predict the moose will enter. One last thing: It's always important to verify in what direction the wind is blowing to avoid letting the moose catch a whiff of your scent.

CHAPTER 7

THE ART OF CALLING

Moose calling is a topic that's been analyzed and discussed from every possible angle. And yet, numerous are the hunters who are still looking for answers to their questions: What's the best way to call? Should I call males or females, dominant bulls or more submissive ones? I'd say that the majority of hunters hesitate before calling, unsure what kind of call will provoke a reaction and get the moose to approach them. Moreover, hunters want to learn to call with confidence, they want to learn how to truly master the art of calling. I myself have experienced such uncertainty and know what it is to question my calling abilities. However, after spending so many years observing moose in their natural habitat, I've come up with a few answers of my own.

EVERYTHING YOU NEED TO KNOW ABOUT CALLING

There are two traditional ways of calling: With your hands or with a moose-calling horn (available in specialty shops). You can also use electronic devices that allow you to play back previously recorded moose calls.

If, like me, you prefer to call the good old-fashioned way, cup your hands around your mouth, pinch your nose with your index fingers and take a deep breath. The important thing to remember is that the call should come from your stomach, not your throat. Press your tongue to the roof of your mouth, contract your abdominal muscles and release the air from your lungs. Practice outdoors (ideally in a forest) by placing a recorder 15 m (50 ft.) away from you and recording your calls. Don't get discouraged, and remember that, as with anything, practice makes perfect. Learning how to call requires discipline and intense training sessions all year round. A lot of hunters master their calls at home and then falter once they enter the forest; they're unsure of what notes to hit or how often they should call. To avoid such mistakes, you need to listen to moose vocalizations over and over and over again, practicing your calls non-stop throughout the year until they become second nature. It took me two years to master my calls. During those two years, I regularly listened to moose calls, hoping to train my ear and learn how to imitate them as perfectly as possible. Of course, some calls are harder to master than others, while others, like young males (OOAHF) and females (UuUuhf), are much easier.

In my experience, the problem with many hunters is that their calls lack moaning. Moaning is an important aspect when it comes to reproducing a moose's call. Females really sound like they're wailing. Make sure your wails come from your gut, not your throat, but remember that doing so requires a constant effort on your part. It's also important to produce vibrations and modulations with your voice when calling.

It's unrealistic to think that there is a miraculous call, one that will guarantee a moose will come running every time you use it. Personally, I think most calls have the potential to be successful.

The language of moose is composed of a variety of sounds, allowing them to communicate with one another using vocalizations that often sound the same, but that have very different meanings—much like ours. Vocal range and register varies from one moose to another, so obtaining the "perfect" pitch is nearly impossible. If your call doesn't work, it's likely because the moose aren't receptive or that there aren't any within earshot.

My numerous expeditions throughout Canada allowed me to conduct valuable research on moose calling. After several years spent observing moose, mainly in the Lac-Mégantic region near the Canada-US border, I realized that the behaviour of moose fluctuates, much like that of humans. The same call can yield very different results from one day to the next.

It's important to understand that moose hunting has greatly evolved over the years; moose have become increasingly wary of hunters.

A lot of hunters call any which way, without really understanding the meaning of the sounds they're emitting. These unusual sounds end up causing moose to be more fearful. The more authentic your calls are, the higher your chances of a successful hunt.

THE DIFFERENT MOOSE CALLS

YOUNG MALE: OOAHF

ADULT MALE: Wrouahf

RECEPTIVE FEMALE: UUuuuuhf

PLAINTIVE FEMALE: Wwaaaaaaaahf

NON-RECEPTIVE FEMALE: MmoAAAhfff MOHF MOHF MOAaaaAHFAaaahf

Listen to the different calls on the Internet (www.youtube.com/watch?v=DbVxUmevOUI) or on my DVD (available at www.hommepanache.ca).

A REAL-LIFE STORY

I've made mistakes, just like you. Although perhaps "mistakes" are just "experiences that didn't work out the first time around." All my "mistakes" have led me to question myself, pushed me to try new things. One of these "mistakes" occurred in 1995 on the first morning of bow-hunting season in the Louise Gosford controlled harvesting zone in the Eastern Townships. I was confident, excited and focused–just like every hunter is at the start of a new hunting season. After a solid hour and a half of making female calls, a cow appeared 200 or 250 m (656 or 820 ft.) away from where I stood. A male was trailing behind her, following her scent. I was blown away by the male's immense rack–it must have measured 140 cm (55 in.) across. These palmate antlers were incredibly huge, I mean each one must have easily measured 30 cm (1 ft.). And the points on this guy–there were so many! With just a few more calls, I was thinking I would be able to convince this impressive bull that a receptive female was just a few hundred metres away. Now this was late September, the start of rut season, and this bull was probably eager to tend to the first receptive female he came across, so I figured that getting him to come my way wouldn't be too difficult. I therefore continued calling with confidence and ease. When his indifference became apparent, I responded with even more fervour and conviction. From time to time, the male would cease courting the female he was with to look up, only to immediately return his attention to his female. He heard my calls, but nothing could get him to give up on the female he was after. I tried as hard as I could to increase my wails, hoping to get the bull to saunter over to me, but to no avail. After a few minutes, the two love-birds slowly wandered off, taking with them any hope I had of scoring a trophy bull. Desperate, I continued to call for the better part of an hour, but with no success. What had I done wrong? Why hadn't I managed to attract that male's attention?

From that day forward, I started to experiment with different tactics, analyzing the reactions of every moose I came across. I quickly realized that no matter where I happened to be, the reactions I provoked were almost always the same.

MALE CALLS VS. FEMALE CALLS

In my opinion, any call can be a successful one. However, the most successful call is usually a male call. Now, don't get me wrong–I'm not saying that if you install yourself in your lookout in the wee hours of the morning and start calling for bulls, they'll all come running! What I am saying is that if a male is within earshot of your call, there's a better chance he'll answer the call of another male rather than the call of a female. When you're in the forest, you can't predict whether your calls will be heard, or if they're heard, whether they'll been heard by a female, a young or mature bull, or a bull that's accompanied by a cow.

By imitating a male call, one thing is for sure: If a male is within earshot, your call will intrigue him, regardless of whether he's a dominant bull or a young male, or if he's alone or accompanied. In this regard, male calls are somewhat universal, efficient in any situation. Of course, I do also practice female calls. In fact, I frequently alternate between male and female calls, as doing so sounds more natural, less suspicious. However, it's important to note that once I've caught a male's attention, I switch over entirely to male calls.

A MALE'S CALL

I believe that a male call is more successful when it comes to attracting a male for two reasons. First off, a male in the presence of one or more ovulating females will rarely leave in search of another female. Of course, it's not impossible, especially near the end of rut season when a male's chances of breeding start to diminish. In general, your chances of attracting a male's attention are increased five-fold if you play the male-calling card.

Secondly, compared to a female's call, a male's call is always effective at drawing a bull's attention, no matter what point in the season you're at. When you imitate a male call, you confront him, provoke him or make him jealous, and if he's a younger bull, you fuel his curiosity.

As rut season nears, mature bulls become territorial and possessive. They group together and confront one another in order to establish where they all stand in the hierarchy. Females, on the other hand, are not yet receptive and haven't started to call out to demonstrate their presence. For this reason, don't bother with female calls at this point in the season.

When rut season is at its peak, an accompanied male is usually indifferent to calls as he has no interest in leaving the female he is courting. If another female is interested in him, he expects her to come to him, not the other way around. So, once again, a female's cry is not your best option at this point. By opting for a male call, you're bound to make an accompanied bull jealous. Fearful of losing his female, he'll be ready to confront whatever male dares to try to steal her. It's the hunting equivalent of breaking into another man's home to steal his wife!

The best time to use a female call is when rut season is over. At this point in the season, males are aware that their chances of breeding are dwindling, thus causing them to act much less indifferently. At this point, it's much more probable to see a male approach a female in the hopes of experiencing a few more moments of ecstasy.

In retrospect, I think that what I should have done to attract the bull that got away was imitate a male's call while walking in his direction, thus making him fearful of losing his female.

A FEMALE'S CALL

A female's call is great for locating a male. A female's call is more far-reaching than a male's muffled "Wrouahf" call.

However, regardless of how far-reaching it is, a female's call is not always effective when it comes to attracting and harvesting a moose, especially if said moose is accompanied by one or more females. In fact, a male often answers a female's call without ever changing locations. Once you've located your target, communicate with him in his own language. In this case, yet again, a male's call would be your best bet.

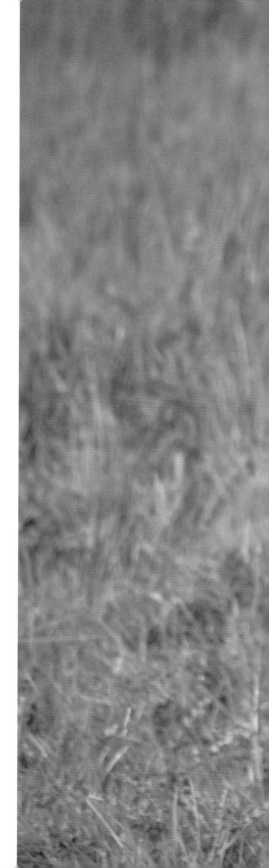

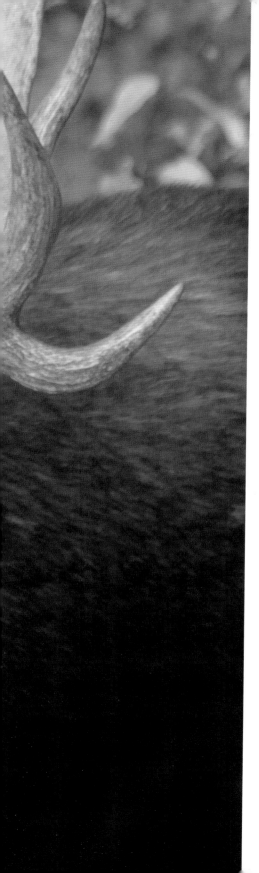

YOUNG MALE CALLS VS. DOMINANT MALE CALLS

I often get asked if it's best to make the sound of a mature bull or that of a younger male, especially when a young male is present.

Personally, I recommend always using a dominant male's "Wrouahf" call. Many hunters think that if they opt for a dominant call, younger males will fearfully stay away. Not true! Young males are curious by nature and when they hear a dominant cry they'll almost always approach, not to confront the other moose, but simply out of curiosity. However, their curiosity has its limits, and usually they won't get any closer than 30 m (100 ft.) from where the call came from–but that's close enough for you to get a clear shot!

By opting for a dominant male call, not only will you pique the curiosity of the younger bulls, you'll provoke the older ones. Basically, this type of call works regardless of whether you're dealing with young or dominant bulls. I refrain from using young male calls simply because mature males don't usually react to this kind of call–if they don't feel threatened or challenged, they'll usually remain pretty indifferent.

The universal call

Remember, no matter the month, no matter whether you're dealing with a solitary or accompanied bull and no matter whether said bull is young or mature, a male's call is usually your best bet when it comes to provoking him or piquing his curiosity. And once you've gotten his attention, all that's left to do is to get him to come within shooting range!

UNDERSTANDING
A FEMALE'S LANGUAGE

Throughout the years, I've come to realize that a female's wail differs from one cow to the next and depends on her period of ovulation. Furthermore, a solitary female typically does not make the same sounds as when she is accompanied by a male. Of course, these are just my observations–remember that just as with all animal behaviour, nothing is set in stone. The following calls are some of the most common, but they can still differ slightly from time to time.

THE MOST COMMON FEMALE CALLS

• An available female hoping to attract the attention of a male has an unwavering wail that lasts approximately four or five seconds. The intervals between calls are rather long and sound like: "WwaaaaaaaaAHFF" "WwaaaaaaaaAHFF."

• At the start of rut season, a female's cries are generally longer and more plaintive as ovulation nears.

• An ovulating female who is tended to by a bull (and for whom ovulation lasts no more than two days) emits a much different sound. Her cries are more subdued and sound like: "UuUuhf" "UuuUUUUuuuhf." They're repeated over and over again and last approximately two to three seconds.

• An non-receptive female usually sounds off in a much more distinct and unique way. The intensity of her wails gradually increases if a courting male is persistent, becoming much more forceful and repetitive. It sounds like: "MMOOOOnonnoo, oooonooffMoon MoOnf." I once counted hundreds of wails within a five-minute period. Once her warning wails finally succeeded in driving her stubborn suitor away, her lamentations slowly tapered off. This kind of protest gets the attention of other males. A far-off male will hear her cries and will hurry to get to her, knowing full well she is not alone, but eager to prove his dominance. In my experience, such cries are the most effective for attracting a dominant male.

If I am Stand hunting, I often start by imitating a non-accompanied female in heat: "WwaaaaaaaaAHFF" "WwaaaaaaaaAHFF." I do this for the first 30 minutes, then switch to the sound of a male meeting up with her: "Wrouahf." Finally, I finish by imitating a protesting female: "MmOAAAHFAAAAAAHF MOAHF MOAHF MOAaaAHFAaaaaaAHF." In most cases, a male shows up by the third set of calls, which are much more pronounced. Hunters need to constantly ask themselves how moose communicate with one another in the forest. They need to know that communication and interaction is never the same in September–it changes all the time. It all depends on how receptive the female is and how patient the male is. For example, if a female desires a male, this does not necessarily mean she will immediately agree to breeding. Knowing that she will be ovulating in the next few days, she wants the male's company. Sometimes, however, the male can become impatient with the female, tired of her protesting wails every time he tries approaching her. The closer the male gets to the female, the louder her wails become. The length of these cries can vary, lasting anywhere between one and seven seconds each. Plus, they're repetitive and can sometimes last for hours. In some instances, a male's patience may run out, causing him to become aggressive towards the female, but he usually calms down quickly, knowing it's useless to rush the female. Switching tactics, the male will begin to court the female, patiently tending to her, assessing her hormonal activity by sniffing her genitals. After several days of courting, the female's short plaintive wails diminish, and she eventually offers herself up to the male.

CALLS THAT GO UNANSWERED

On September 26, 2003, I was in the Yukon; it was late afternoon and the weather was cool, my surroundings still. After having bagged a 152 cm (60 in.) trophy moose with my bow and arrow, I still had two whole days of hunting ahead of me, time I planned to use filming my audio-visual document on moose *The Rack Man in the Yukon 2.*

I made my way over to some magnificent lava flows located at the tip of a lake. The weather was perfect for calling–calm and windless. As I approached the lake, I spotted a cow with her calf and a male with a 152-cm (60-in.) rack. I was about 50 m (165 ft.) from them, and for three hours I watched as the male became increasingly impatient with the female's mounting wails (she sometimes cried out more than 100 times within a five-minute period). Her calls lasted anywhere between one and seven seconds–it was spectacular to see how persistent she was! The more interest the male showed, the more she would protest. It was fascinating listening to her wails echo off the mountaintops–anyone would have been impressed, I'm telling you!

At one point during this ritual, two other males arrived, both a little smaller than the bull accompanying the female. One of the intruders stopped 100 m (330 ft.) from the couple, casually observing his surroundings, all while sizing up his competition. The second male, a tad more daring, got within 20 m (65 ft.). The dominant male, however, would have none of it, and he chased both males away. There was no way he was going to let another male close to his female! The smaller males remained in the area, subtly trying to approach the female from time to time–but getting chased away every time!

I regularly get asked why some calls go unanswered. My answer is always that nature speaks for itself. It's normal for some calls to go unanswered, even if there are moose in the area.

For example, one year I was on my hunting ground, observing my salt licks from my watchtower. A female was just a few metres from where I stood, wailing in the hopes of attracting a male. More than 30 minutes went by and nothing happened. After about an hour, a male quietly sauntered over, stopping just 300 m (328 yards) from where the female and I stood. Neither the male nor the female noticed my presence–I was an invisible ghost, taking in the beauty of the moment, appreciating these majestic creatures.

"It's normal for some calls to go unanswered, even if you've spotted moose in the area."

So what happened next? Absolutely nothing! For no apparent reason, the male turned around and left without paying any mind to the female desperately trying to get his attention. And yet, it was the peak of rut season and the female was crying out one or two times every ten minutes or so!

The female lingered for approximately three hours, filling up on minerals before heading towards the hillside. Such an occurrence is extremely rare in September, but it can happen. The female had all the qualities for attracting the male, so what exactly happened? Were there other female prospects in the area? Was there a more dominant male nearby who warned the bull I spotted to leave, that he wasn't welcome? Perhaps the male sensed that the female wasn't quite yet ready for breeding? In my opinion, he just wasn't all that interested–simple as that.

Two days later, I returned to the same spot, but this time I called just like the female had before me. After only 20 minutes, I was lucky to harvest a magnificent male with a rack spanning 127 cm (50 in.). The circumstances and the calls were the same, but the outcome was much different from two days earlier. It would be pretentious of me to think that my calls were more convincing than the female's had been. That wasn't the case, of course. The results always depend on how receptive a moose is in that particular moment, and what kind of mood he's in.

In September 2000, I was in the Yukon in one of the wildest places on earth–an area with the highest density of moose. Early in the day, I imitated an accompanied female for over three hours without getting any reply, even though my call was perfect. Looking back, I'm convinced that the moose in the area were either busy tending to a female or too far off to hear my calls, otherwise I would have gotten a response. During rut season, a solitary male will normally show his face within 30 minutes of hearing a call. Regardless of whether you use a female or male call, you should get an answer . . . except in rare cases like the one I just described.

TRAINING

I regularly offer training sessions on how to call and hunt moose. Visit my website for more details:

www.hommepanache.ca

CHAPTER 8

THE "RIGHT" WAY
TO HUNT MOOSE

Over the years, I've met with many hunters who were hoping, almost desperately, to discover the ultimate hunting secret, the one that'll change the way they hunt forever. They expect me to teach them a precise, unwavering technique, one they'll be able to use in any situation. Does such a technique exist? Absolutely not! My experience has taught me that a good hunter needs to take into account numerous factors, in addition to mastering different calling techniques and using a little logic.

I've always believed that the best way to hunt a moose is to replicate his behaviour as accurately as possible, thus putting him at ease and erasing any suspicions he may have with regards to you. Don't waste your time (and lose your breath!) calling without doing anything else. Think about it. When a moose is approaching you, you hear not only his call, but also his movements—the rustling leaves, the sound of his antlers thrashing against a tree—you know when he stops to take a break. I take all these factors into account when I'm approaching a moose. You need to see the full picture, not just the sum of its parts.

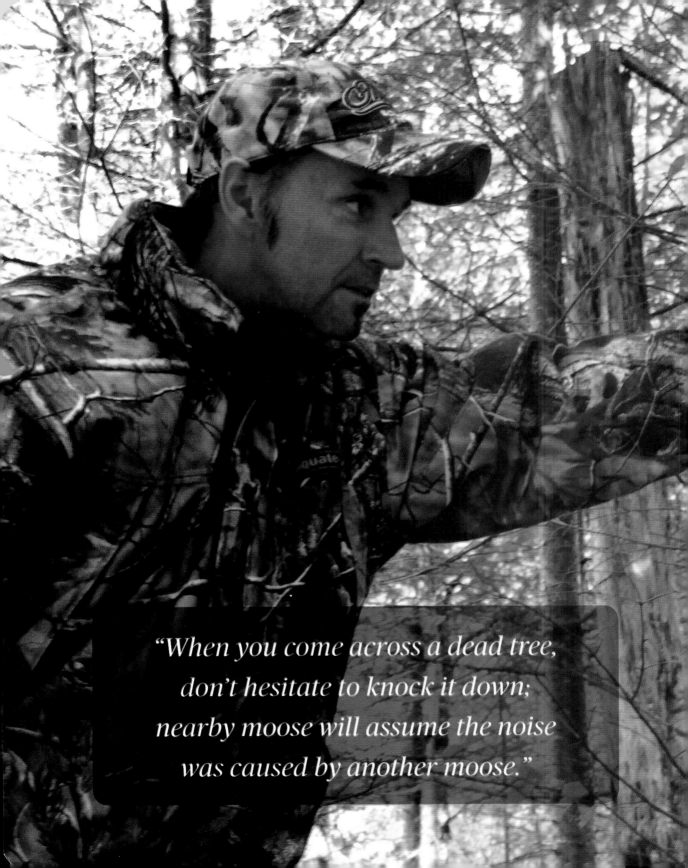

"When you come across a dead tree, don't hesitate to knock it down; nearby moose will assume the noise was caused by another moose."

APPROACHING YOUR TARGET

All the traditional methods are fine for tracking a moose. You can locate a moose simply by navigating the forest by foot, vehicle or canoe. You can also try calling or rattling, or a combination of both while practicing your Spot-and-Stalk hunting techniques. You can follow the cries of a non-receptive female (a female not yet ready to mate) as this is usually a good indicator that a male is close by trying to win her over. What's very important when approaching a moose is determining whether he is alone or accompanied by one or several females. In some cases, it's easy to confirm whether or not a male is accompanied as you'll see a group of moose roaming the burns or lingering by a lake. In other instances, you need to be more attentive in order to hear whether a female is crying out in protest, letting the male who just answered you know that he isn't welcome. Either way, the important thing to remember is that from this point on, you'll need to include some male calls in your repertoire in order to convince your opponent that you're another male ready to confront him.

WHY IS IT IMPORTANT TO KNOW WHETHER A MALE IS ACCOMPANIED OR NOT?

Simply because it will allow you to adopt the appropriate technique.

If the male is alone, you can safely assume he'll walk towards you. However, you have to be ready to meet him halfway. In the wild, here's how it works: One moose takes a few steps, stops and waits while the second moose takes a few steps. And back and forth and back and forth it goes–it's just the way it works with solitary moose. Knowing this, don't waste your time staying in one spot–it's much more natural if you move around!

If a male is already accompanied by one or several females, he'll usually answer your call but will be hesitant to leave his harem to come meet you. In his mind, there's no point in confronting you just yet–you're still too far away to be considered an imminent threat. In situations like this, you need to approach him with confidence and self-assurance, all while constantly emitting male calls and making rattling noises. Slowly advance in a straight line until you're about 60 m (200 ft.) from your target. Remember that a male who's in the presence of females will not feel threatened by another male until a visual contact is established.

One step at a time

Approaching a moose is a two-step process. One: You need to get within 60 m (200 ft.) of the animal; and two: You need to get your target within shooting range. I say 60 m (200 ft.), but it can vary between 40 and 90 m (130 to 300 ft.), depending on the lay of the land–in some cases you might not get a clear shot at your target unless you're 45 m (150 ft.) away; in other cases you can be as far as 90 m (300 ft.) away and be just fine. Steadily advance in a straight line until you're within shooting range. Slowly make your way towards your target, all the while making light rattling sounds and imitating the male's grunt. Take the time to stop every so often, listening to see if the male is making his way towards you.

GETTING A REACTION

Over the years, I've experimented with and perfected my rattling technique. I have harvested many moose, and have helped other hunters harvest many moose, sometimes using nothing but branches to reproduce the rattling sound. One particular harvest stands out in my mind, not only because I managed to outwit the stunning creature, but because my cameraman captured the whole thing on tape. It was spectacular!

It was in 2003 in the Yukon, with the outfitter company MacMillan River Adventures. My client and I had already bagged our quota (in addition to one grizzly), but still had four days left in our hunting trip. The outfitter's taxidermist, Bob Paul, had yet to harvest his moose, so I offered to guide him. A few days prior, I had located an imposing bull accompanied by a female. When we spotted them, they were approximately 300 m (328 yards) from where we stood. I approached them, emitting male cries and rattling. The male immediately re acted and began to make his way towards me, his antlers thrashing about. All of a sudden, he stopped and just stood there, observing me. Visual contact was made and it was clear that I was not welcome on his territory. I watched as he started towards me again, thrashing his head from side to side. I immediately began imitating him, using my paddle as antlers. Not only was he tossing his head, but his eyes were bulging and his ears dropped. It was amazing to watch and a thrill to experience. Our confrontation led us to within 12 m (40 ft.) of one another. I can still see him, tossing his impressive 147-cm (58-in.) rack back and forth. He had a branch caught in his antlers and as he strolled around us, displaying his grandeur for all to see, we realized that the branch was obstructing his kill zone. Luckily, the branch was precariously hanging, seconds away from falling. As soon as the branch unhinged itself–bam!–our shooter released his arrow and down went the beast! What an incredible memory!

With Bob Paul and his trophy male.
Bob stars in The Rack Man's movie *The Grizzly and the Moose.*

I chose to share this story with you in order to illustrate the importance of visual staging when hunting. You can use an actual moose pallet, although I don't recommend it. To be successful, you have to use a rack at least 1 m (40 in.) wide, which tends to be quite heavy. A face-off with a bull can last anywhere between 5 and 40 minutes, so chances are you'll be extremely exhausted from holding up such a large rack for so long–and if you lower it, even for just a second, you risk losing the bull entirely.

I recommend using a paddle or a light imitation pallet like the one I designed and marketed. Ultimately, the important thing is that you present something that looks as close to the real deal as possible.

A TRIED-AND-TESTED TECHNIQUE

As a rule, whenever I spot a male, I communicate with him with grunts, all while slowly advancing towards him, much in the same way a fellow bull would. As much as possible, I try moving against the wind, so that my odour does not catch up to my prey before I do. I rub my rattling pallet in the trees as I walk, stopping occasionally to vigorously rub it against the bark, as this is how a bull trying to intimidate a rival bull acts in the wild.

I never hide when I get within a bull's field of vision. On the contrary, I make myself all the more visible by raising my rattling pallet to my forehead, replicating the silhouette of a moose, while remaining in a shaded area. This way, the moose is unable to clearly see me, but is able to see a vague outline of something that looks like a potential rival. Trust me, this strategy, a true reproduction of what happens in the wild, will pique your target's curiosity and encourage him to confront you from a closer distance.

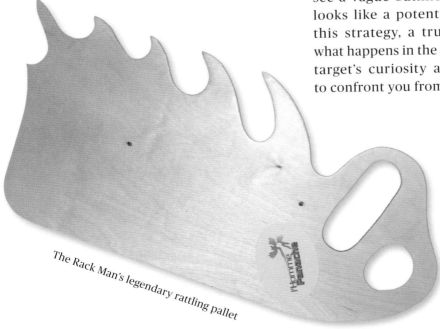

The Rack Man's legendary rattling pallet

MICKAËL BOLDUC: 15 YEARS OLD AND ALREADY THREE MOOSE UNDER HIS BELT

The story of a young man turned passionate hunter comes to mind. The young man's name is Mickaël Bolduc and he comes from Rouyn-Noranda. At just 13 years old, he decided he wanted to start hunting. He attended one of my conferences and enrolled in one of my training sessions with his father.

The following season, he headed out with his father in search of his first harvest. Following my advice and armed with a rifle and the will to succeed (and a little luck!), he harvested his very first moose–an impressive 1 ½-year-old moose. The next year, he killed his second moose. And finally, believe it or not, the following year Mickaël harvested his third trophy, this time using a bow and arrow!

I met up with the young hunter again during my 2006 tour, and he excitedly recounted every detail of his latest harvest. He explained that he had been calling, alternating between male and female cries. Eventually, not only did he hear a male answer back, but he noticed some far-off female sounds as well. When he realized that the male appeared indifferent to him, unwilling to come to him, Mickaël began to slowly make his way towards the male. Walking at a steady pace, he headed in the couple's direction, all while practicing the techniques I had taught him three years earlier: Advance slowly, as a moose would do, alternate between male and female calls, do a bit of rattling against trees and shrubs, etc. As he neared, he quickly realized that he was coming upon not two, but six moose: Four females and two males! He continued to close in on the group, reproducing the behaviour of a male and regularly emitting a "Wrouahf" here and there. Before he knew it, he was about 15 m away (approximately 50 ft.) from one of the males. Despite the short distance that separated him from the male, he was unable to get a clear shot–either the male was facing him or the trees were in the way or a female would saunter over between him and the bull. Mickaël remained focused and patient, continuing to behave and communicate like a bull. After about 30 minutes, he was finally able to shoot an arrow directly into the kill zone of one of the males–a much deserved trophy!

FACE-TO-FACE WITH YOUR PREY

Each year, my conferences allow me to meet with thousands of hunters of all ages. During these meetings, I've had the privilege of talking with hunters who, like me, hunt with a bow or crossbow, and one question always seems to come up: How do you convince a hesitant male to get close enough for you to hit his kill zone?

Generally speaking, most hunters have no problem getting a male to answer their calls and approach within 100 m (328 ft.) of them. However, when the moose gets closer to the hunter, that's when things get tricky. A lot of hunters (perhaps due to inexperience) get nervous when a moose approaches them and are unsure of how to react. I see the same thing happen over and over again: The bull stands immobile about 60 m (200 ft.) from the hunter—a distance still too great for any hunter to hope to hit a moose's kill zone with his arrow. In such cases, you need to convince your target, both vocally and visually, that you are an adversary looking to court the females in the area and are ready to fight him in order to do so. By acting this way, you'll be inciting him to close the psychological (and physical) gap still separating you from the kill.

In my early conference days, hunters were always surprised to hear me telling them to make noise when approaching a moose. Several, if not the majority of hunters, call and then go to great lengths not to make any noise, standing perfectly still, thinking this is the only way to not scare off an animal. But when you stop to think about it, this isn't a very logical way to go about it. You call in the hopes of sounding like a moose (and thus hope to attract a moose), and then when a moose does show up, you make no effort to convince him you are, in fact, a moose. And hunters wonder why most creatures stall 60 or 90 m (200 or 300 ft.) away from them! I have been a fan of hunting since adolescence, and when I first started hunting, I listened attentively to the advice of more experienced hunters. According to them, it was important to make as little noise as possible when approaching a moose. I followed this advice for many years, feeling increasingly frustrated (just like many of the hunters who attend my conferences) every time I was unable to harvest a bull I had managed to draw in with my calls.

THE MOMENT
THAT CHANGED IT ALL

In was September 1990. I was in the Maganasipi controlled harvesting zone in Témiscamingue. It had been a cold, long night and the sun was just starting to stretch its first rays across the sky. It was 7:30 in the morning and I was nearing the end of my expedition. I was scheduled to leave the very next day and the panic was starting to settle in–I was already picturing myself heading home empty handed. A few days prior, I had spotted tracks that appeared to belong to an imposing bull.

Heaving my bow across my shoulder, I decided to do one final tour of the forest, retracing my steps back to the area where I had seen those impressive tracks. The scenery was breathtaking–the trees aflame with colour. The sun was piercing the treetops, a sharp contrast to the layer of white frost covering the earth like a blanket.

I was strolling through the area, taking in all its beauty, when I suddenly spotted

fresh tracks in the earth. Shaking myself from my reverie, I realized the tracks were a sure indication that a moose had recently passed through the area. Getting a hold of myself, I decided to try a few dominant male calls: "Wrouahf, Wrouahf." After about 30 repetitions, I finally got a response from what I believed to be a rather large male. His sombre cry echoed between the mountaintops, appearing to be no more than 500 m (547 yards) away. I continued

calling. Shivering in anticipation, I answered every one of his calls. I continued walking until I reached an ancient logging site, an area now frequently visited by moose.

Approximately ten minutes later, I spotted him. He was just 50 or so metres from me (165 ft.), but the forest's bush density was obstructing my view of him. He stood motionless, seeming to disappear into the background, even though I knew he

was still very much there! All activity ceased and I was afraid of calling. I was afraid of his picking up on some abnormality. So I waited. Several minutes went by and still nothing. I was just standing there, wondering what to do next, knowing I was in no position to shoot. My mind was reeling. Eventually I decided to move, hoping to get a better shot. My movements began to stir the branches, causing much more noise than I had anticipated. All I could think was, "Great, these sounds are bound to scare him off!"

Suddenly, an idea came to mind: I decided to reproduce my calls in the hopes of masking some of the noises my movements were making. To my immense surprise, the bull answered back! He thought I was another male, strolling through the area.

I slowly advanced towards him, catching glimpses of his majestic rack glimmering in the sun. He scoured the area with his eyes, left, right, listening for any hint of sound, then suddenly started down the path leading in my direction. He stopped 20 m (65 ft.) shy of where I stood. He was scanning the area, seeking me out, determined to find the imposter. He was facing me, making it impossible for me to shoot. I was standing, immobile, near a maple tree, staying as still and as silent as possible. The silence stretched on for another minute or so, and then the moose decided to continue on his way, calling to make his presence known, yet oblivious to the fact that these were the last steps he would ever take.

Slowly, steadily, I arched my bow. My trophy, with his impressive 130 cm (50 in.) rack, was now just 10 m (32 ft.) away. He stopped in his tracks, staring at me with his dark eyes one last time. He was so close, and yet I still couldn't shoot as his shoulder was obstructing my view of his vital organs. Twenty excruciating seconds ticked by. My heart was beating so wildly, I was convinced he could hear it!

All of a sudden, he slowly stepped over a fallen pine tree, knocked over by the wind. Now was my chance! I heard the impact of my arrow as it pierced his lungs so deeply only the feathers at the tip of the arrow could still be seen. Taken aback by the pain, the bull arched his back and started to gallop away. A few metres later my trophy bull collapsed in a heap next to a large boulder. This experience taught me that you should never stop calling, regardless of the call (male or female).

"In my early conference days, hunters were always surprised to hear me telling them to make noise when approaching a moose."

THE NATURAL BEHAVIOUR OF MOOSE

In order to understand why moose stop every dozen or so metres, you need to first understand what goes on in a forest. It's only after numerous wails from a female that a male will respond. The impatient bull will descend from his perch atop the mountain and follow the female's laments. As he approaches, he'll stop, using his heightened sense of hearing and smell to pinpoint her exact location, then continue on his way.

As he nears her (although he has yet to spot her), he'll stop again, this time for a longer period, and listen attentively. He'll take in all the sounds: Snapping branches, her munching on leaves and sprouts, wailing as she moves about. He'll smell her distinct odour; the smell of rut is in the air. He follows his nose until he finally sees her in the distance. What an incredible scene, brought to you by Mother Nature herself!

THE KEY TO IMITATING MOOSE BEHAVIOUR

Picture yourself hunting: After a few female cries, you've managed to attract your trophy male. He now stands about 75 m (250 ft.) away, although you can't yet see him. Emit a soft female wail, wait five minutes, snap a branch, wait another five to ten minutes, snap another branch and so on and so forth.

It's often during these calling sessions that hunters remain silent for too-long stretches at a time, opting for silence instead of noise. If you imitate a female and then remain silent, chances are any nearby male will quickly lose interest and eventually leave the area. Rifle hunters often used the silent method in the past because when you hunt with a rifle, you don't need to draw the moose in–you can shoot from a much greater distance.

Today, more hunters make bows their weapon of choice, and because of this, hunting has evolved. Hunting with a bow or crossbow means you need to get your prey to come closer to you. If the moose you've spotted stops moving, you need to regularly emit female lamentations interspersed with branch snapping in order to convince him that you're a female eagerly awaiting his arrival.

If the male reacts, stay where you are and stick with your strategy until he is within shooting range.

If the male doesn't react, chances are you're dealing with a more docile creature. His reaction, or rather lack thereof, is simply a sign that he's in no rush to mate.

When this happens, I suggest calling in the opposite direction, away from the male, in the hopes of enticing him to move in your direction. If he still refuses to move, now's the time to do exactly as the female would do–that is wail and move (should you have ample room to do so, of course). To lure the bull to you, you need to walk at an angle in his direction, snapping branches and calling as you go. It's important that the wind be blowing in the right direction so that you can sneak up on the moose without being noticed. Slowly make your way from one grove to another while pulling leaves off branches like a female would if she were stopping to nibble. Call in the direction of the male; stop and wait to see if he reacts.

Still no reaction? You need to reassure him. Under no circumstance should you stop what you're doing.

Be patient –the male might not be feeling pressured in the least. In fact, it's common for a male to wait 15 to 20 minutes before approaching a female. If, after several attempts at trying to imitate a female slowly moving towards him, the male still doesn't budge, I suggest imitating the sound of another male suddenly arriving to claim the female. More often than not, this will encourage your prey to bridge those final few metres, getting close enough for you to shoot.

INTIMIDATING YOUR ADVERSARY

What hunter hasn't seen those famous clips where two dominant males are preparing to confront one another? The moments leading up to a potential fight between two aggressive males are always so captivating to watch. Watching such a scene will allow you to see that when it comes to moose, it all boils down to sizing up and intimidating your adversary. And every time, both parties will do whatever it takes to discourage his

opponent from fighting, meaning these face-offs rarely lead to actual combat. Over the years, I've had the privilege of observing several of these face-offs, allowing me to perfect my own intimidation tactics. Each time I witness two males squaring off, I stay focused, attentive, learning each time from their actions. Here is a step-by-step guide on what to do and how to act in order to convince a bull you're a worthy opponent.

ADAPTING TO YOUR ADVERSARY

First off, it's important to know that moose closely resemble us. Allow me to explain: Much like us humans, no two moose have the same character or personality. This means you never know what to expect when hunting–you could wind up dealing with an aggressive male who will stop at nothing to intimidate you, or you might come face-to-face with a more docile bull. I've tested this premise so many times that I can safely say that a moose's aggression is in no way proportional to the size of his rack. In fact, on more than one occasion, I've premise a young male act much more aggressively than a mature bull would. Therefore, I strongly recommend adapting your temperament to match that of your opponent.

If, for example, a male begins to aggressively rub his pallet against a tree, go ahead and do the same. Why? Simply to convince your opponent that you're a fellow bull and that it's his duty to confront you.

When you get approximately 60 m (200 ft.) from your adversary, both of you observing the other, it's important that you hold up your pallet and act just like him. If your opponent thrashes his antlers against some branches, follow suit, grunting as you do. However, if your opponent is observing you but is showing no signs of aggression, simply do a bit of rattling, followed by a few grunts. In all probability, you're dealing with a more docile male and it's your job to convince him that you're there to confront him.

At this point, you're still in the early stages of intimidation, so it's important to display your pallet when stopping to observe your opponent. The fact that the bull makes out what appears to be the rack of another male, confirms to him that he is, indeed, looking at a potential rival. Of course, it's important to note that brandishing a rattling pallet, arms extended, is not enough–you also need to adopt the movements that go with it.

SLOWLY STRUTTING ABOUT

At this point, you need to start swinging your pallet back and forth, exactly like a male on the verge of fighting would. This swinging movement flaunts the size of your rack and serves to intimidate an opponent. When confronting one another, males will often turn sideways and circle their opponent. As I already mentioned, it's essential that you adapt to the temperament of the animal you're confronting. Adapting doesn't just mean toying with your pallet, it means being patient, taking your time and not jumping the gun.

A mistake that a lot of hunters make is thinking (wrongfully so) that the whole approach process takes but a few minutes.

Your opponent needs to be confident, and this can take time. It can take 10, 20, 40 minutes (sometimes longer) to get within shooting range of your target. Don't worry about how long it takes– what's important is holding your own against your adversary.

ADMIRING YOUR PREY

Move sideways just like your opponent, facing him at all times. When your adversary begins to strut around in this manner, he's doing so in order to flaunt his mass, giving you a moment to take in the size of his rack. Do not get your arrow ready just yet. On the contrary, take your time. Admire your opponent. If everything goes as planned, his next move should be his final one, and before you know it, he'll be within shooting range. Don't forget that a moose in combat mode is usually a dead moose.

You're not wrong to think that some bulls are so determined to impress their adversary that nothing will deter them. I once confronted an impressive male, drawing him within shooting range, my eyes locked with his. But, because I had no desire to kill him and we had captured enough footage for the scene, I ceased my intimidation tactics. Well, believe it or not, the bull continued to approach me, despite all my cries imploring him to stop. He was literally on autopilot, with only one goal in mind: To intimidate me.

THE FINAL SECONDS BEFORE SHOOTING

If the male swerves to the left, you need to imitate him by turning to the right and slowly making your way towards him. But remember: It's important, essential even, that you keep your pallet high above your head so that your opponent continues to think you're a fellow moose. Always walk sideways, your eyes never leaving your prey, swinging your pallet from side to side. This way, not only will you look more credible to your opponent, but you'll be able to constantly keep an eye on him, which will allow you to easily replicate his movements. You'll quickly be able to predict his next move as he'll repeat the same actions over and over again. It's up to you to analyze your opponent's moves, commit them to memory–they'll be crucial in deciding when and where to shoot your arrow.

At this point in the face-off, you should be within 45 m (150 ft.) of your prey. Of course, this may vary depending on the lay of the land. You can easily harvest a moose from a distance of 30 m (100 ft.), but why not prolong the pleasure? Wait until you've managed to get the bull within 15 m (50 ft.)–you'll see, it's quite a thrill!

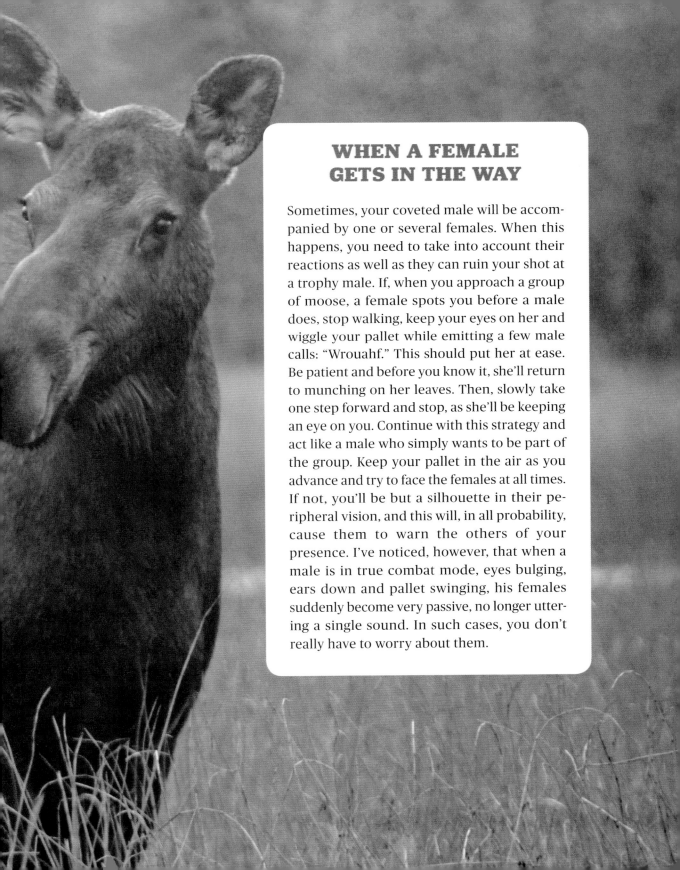

WHEN A FEMALE GETS IN THE WAY

Sometimes, your coveted male will be accompanied by one or several females. When this happens, you need to take into account their reactions as well as they can ruin your shot at a trophy male. If, when you approach a group of moose, a female spots you before a male does, stop walking, keep your eyes on her and wiggle your pallet while emitting a few male calls: "Wrouahf." This should put her at ease. Be patient and before you know it, she'll return to munching on her leaves. Then, slowly take one step forward and stop, as she'll be keeping an eye on you. Continue with this strategy and act like a male who simply wants to be part of the group. Keep your pallet in the air as you advance and try to face the females at all times. If not, you'll be but a silhouette in their peripheral vision, and this will, in all probability, cause them to warn the others of your presence. I've noticed, however, that when a male is in true combat mode, eyes bulging, ears down and pallet swinging, his females suddenly become very passive, no longer uttering a single sound. In such cases, you don't really have to worry about them.

THE RIGHT SPOT

No matter from what distance you want to harvest your kill, you first need to determine the right spot and angle from which to shoot. To do so, you need to analyze the space separating you from your target. If you remembered to calculate the number of steps your prey takes before taking a break or changing directions, you should be in a position to anticipate his next move and determine ahead of time what *your* next move should be.

THE RIGHT TIME

Once you've made up your mind, all that's left to do is continue with your strategy and, a few seconds before shooting, when your prey is no longer analyzing you and instead is moving about, you can quietly lay your pallet on the ground. Draw your bow as the male passes between the trees or nears a clearing. Next, surprise him with a female call–"Moahf"–and your prey is as good as dead!

As I mentioned before, when a male is in confrontation mode, he's so focused that he no longer sees or hears anything. So, even if you take the time to drop your pallet on the ground, your prey will be oblivious. In addition to pushing the experience to the maximum and succeeding in drawing your target so close, you'll have the chance to shoot your arrow directly in your target's kill zone. It goes without saying that getting a moose to approach you after engaging him in combat mode is awe-inspiring, but it's imperative that you keep your emotions in check. You need to remember that you're the one in charge.

DON'T PANIC

I can already hear some of you saying, "Langlois is completely crazy! He actually believes that I'll risk getting charged by a moose, all in the name of hunting!" To which I would have to say that, yes, there is a risk of a moose charging at you, but it's a very small one. Each situation is unique and it's up to you to judge the risks.

If a moose ever decides to charge at you, he'll give you ample warning. His physical appearance will betray his intentions; he'll flatten his ears back, widen his eyes and the hairs on the back of his neck and shoulders will stand up. At this point, he's likely to be around 6 m (20 ft.) from you, meaning you probably had at least one clear shot. If that isn't the case, don't put it off any longer–shoot now. I've harvested moose a few times like this, and each time it's a major adrenaline rush. If ever you have the chance to experience such a rush, you'll definitely come home feeling elated!

REMEMBER

A moose in combat mode is usually
a dead moose. In other words, he's
yours for the taking. Don't forget it!

THE HARVEST

Regardless of the hunting weapon you choose to use, it's imperative that you have a clear shot of the moose's kill zone before shooting, otherwise you run the risk of simply injuring him and never seeing him again. For a fatal shot, aim for the lungs, the liver or the heart. If you hunt with a bow or crossbow, don't shoot until you're sure of hitting your target in the back of his shoulder.

It's extremely rare for a moose to immediately collapse after being shot. Generally speaking, once he's been hit, he'll run off. Wait about an hour before going after him so as not to startle him even more, unless, of course, you saw him collapse.

In Quebec, when a hunter kills a moose, he is required to attach a transport coupon from his licence onto the animal's body, as well as the coupon of the hunter who accompanied him on the expedition (see page 37). The coupons must be attached on the day of the harvest.

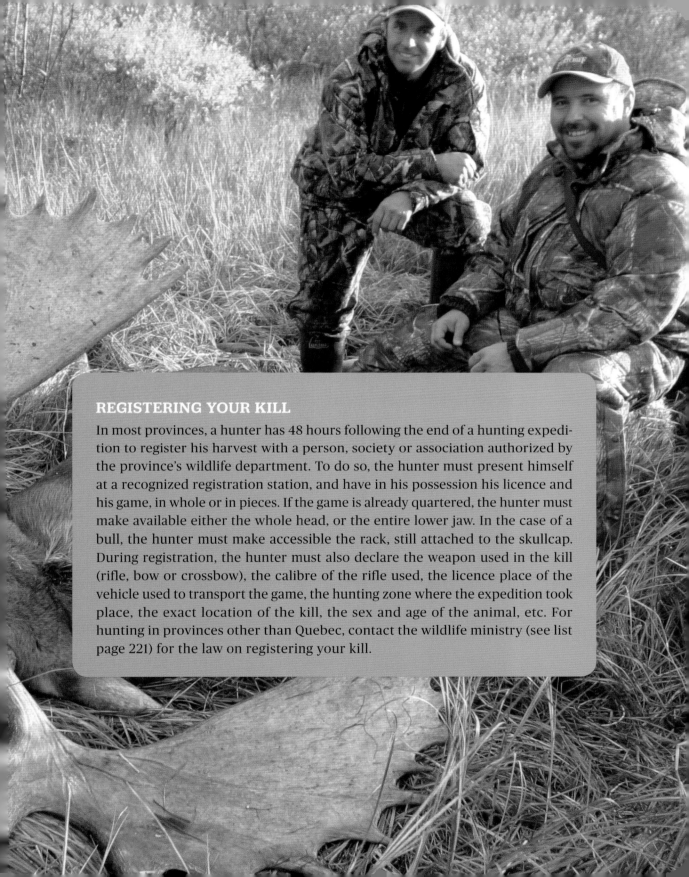

REGISTERING YOUR KILL

In most provinces, a hunter has 48 hours following the end of a hunting expedition to register his harvest with a person, society or association authorized by the province's wildlife department. To do so, the hunter must present himself at a recognized registration station, and have in his possession his licence and his game, in whole or in pieces. If the game is already quartered, the hunter must make available either the whole head, or the entire lower jaw. In the case of a bull, the hunter must make accessible the rack, still attached to the skullcap. During registration, the hunter must also declare the weapon used in the kill (rifle, bow or crossbow), the calibre of the rifle used, the licence place of the vehicle used to transport the game, the hunting zone where the expedition took place, the exact location of the kill, the sex and age of the animal, etc. For hunting in provinces other than Quebec, contact the wildlife ministry (see list page 221) for the law on registering your kill.

CHAPTER 9

ALL ABOUT RUT PITS

Starting around September 7th and during the weeks leading up to rut season, bulls dedicate a lot of their time to preparing rut pits to attract females. They'll continue making pits for weeks, increasing their efforts during the peak of the rut season (between September 18th and October 5th). Keep in mind that dates can vary by over a week across the country.

Rut pits are usually found along bodies of water, in areas abundant with foliage and coniferous trees where females can stock up on food. I've stumbled upon rut pits in some water holes surrounded by huge fir and spruce trees and covered in wild holly where a green, spongy layer covers the ground. In my experience, I'd say that 60% of rut pits are dug near bodies of water, in areas where the soil is humid and soft. Approximately 30% of rut pits can be found in logging areas and clearings, and 10% on mountaintops.

THE MATING RITUAL

Picture this: A moose appears at the edge of the forest and suddenly begins to scrape the ground with his hooves, creating a depression over which he urinates. He repeats this synchronized routine 20 times or so and then rubs the thick, pungent mixture onto his fur and antlers. Using his massive hooves, he splashes the mud and rubs his head in it. Next, he lies in the pit he's made, coating his entire body in the mixture. The mixture's strong scent attracts cows in heat like moths to a flame. But why does the male go to all that trouble?

A lone male usually uses rut pits to try to attract females. If he's already accompanied by females, this ritual allows him to attract even more! A rut pit, also called a wallow, can be up to 30 cm (1 ft.) deep and is about 50 cm to 1 m (1 ft. 7 in. to 3 ft. 3 in.) wide. It's important to note that the size of a rut pit is in no way proportional to its ability to attract females.

A bull will stop at nothing to protect his rut pit, even going so far as to spar with another bull, as this is the area where his honeymoon is set to take place. He'll guard the area, staying within 500 m (547 yards) of his wallow, all while listening attentively for the cries of a female in heat. The strong scent of the rut pit will attract females, and some will even submerge themselves in the pungent pool of urine. This is indicative of a female's receptivity and is usually followed by mating.

Sometimes a rut pit attracts several females at once, which leads to confrontation. When this happens, it stimulates the females' need to breed and a "hormonal hierarchy" naturally occurs. The first female ready to mate stays close to the wallow, warding off the others. Sometimes she'll even urinate in the pit and then submerge herself in the urine while the other females watch from afar, whining and waiting their turn. This is usually when the male shows up and consents to mate two or three times with the first female. He then goes on to mate with the others, sowing his seeds as much possible. If some of the females aren't quite ready for mating, the bull will continue to make his wallows for future females. Once mating season is over, the bull abandons his pits, no longer at all interested in tending to them, and his regular routine of drinking, eating and sleeping takes precedence once again.

TAKING ADVANTAGE OF A RUT PIT

I've had the pleasure of meeting with many hunters over the years, several of whom have told me they were lucky enough to spot a rut pit at least once during their hunting career. Most shared how shocked they were by the smell issuing from the pit. They went on to tell me how they shared their discovery with their friends back at camp. However, when asked if they'd thought to exploit the wallow, almost every single one of them answered that they hadn't! I'd say almost all of them weren't aware of how incredibly beneficial to a hunter a wallow can be.

A fresh rut pit is a true gold mine for a hunter, as it is a very strong indicator that a mature male is within a 500-m (550-yard) radius. What's more, a hunter can use the mud from a rut pit as camouflage–the best kind there is! A good strategy is to use the pit just as a bull would, and that means rolling around in it and covering your clothes with the thick mixture. You can even transfer some of the mixture into a Ziploc bag for future use. Using the mixture from a rut pit completely covers a hunter's natural scent. When you're covered in rut pit mixture, you can approach a moose from any direction without worrying about the wind as the moose will never be able to detect your odour.

RELYING ON THE ODOUR

When you discover a rut pit, use the pungency of its smell to determine how fresh it is.

If the odour is foul and strong-smelling, your chances of spotting a moose are very high. If the rut pit is almost odourless, consider it a sign you should continue scouting the area in search of a fresher pit.

LIVING PROOF

I remember a moose that I harvested back in 1993 in the Louise-Gosford controlled harvesting zone in Lac-Mégantic. I owe that kill entirely to the rut pit odour I was wearing that completely covered up my natural scent. It was one of the first days of the season, the weather was gorgeous and the landscape was breathtaking. The leaves on the trees were bright with colour. I was with my hunting buddy Sylvain. Earlier that morning, after a series of unanswered calls, we decided to head further into the woods to explore. We were following an old logger's trail that I had pinpointed using my topographic map, navigating its long and winding curves in our all-terrain vehicles.

Approximately 1.5 km (nearly 1 mi.) in, we spotted moose tracks heading in our direction, right on the trail. I killed the engine and stooped down to take a closer look at the tracks. They were fresh, which could only mean one thing: the noise of the vehicle had spooked the moose and it had gone running in the opposite direction. I took a moment to consider what the best strategy would be. Looking at my map, I quickly realized that we were right next to the border separating Canada from the United States. Without wasting another second, Sylvain and I headed in that direction for a clearer view of our surroundings.

We suddenly spotted a fresh rut pit along the border. I felt like I had just unearthed a valuable treasure (I always feel that way when I discover a rut pit!). Instinctively, I sat down in the pit. Sylvain, obviously taken aback, yelled that I was acting crazy! I immediately replied that I was not crazy and that he too should roll around in the mud. I knew that by doing so, we were both covering up our natural scent, making us almost invisible to our prey. But just as we were getting ready to stand watch, strong winds and a torrential downpour forced us back to camp.

The next morning, we awoke to clear skies. We immediately headed back to where we had seen the rut pit the day before (unfortunately having no choice but to get there using our all-terrain vehicles). We abandoned our vehicles 750 m (0.5 mi.) from the site, making the rest of the way on foot. Once onsite, Sylvain and I again jumped into the rut pit and rolled around in the pungent mixture.

Knowing that strong winds aren't conducive to calling, we decided to practice our Stand hunting, hoping to come across the moose from the day before. I had a pretty good idea of its location, so I started to lead the way down a small path made by the moose, Sylvain following 15 m (50 ft.) behind. My goal was to stealthily approach the moose and to get as close to it as possible. Thanks to the rut pit mud I was covered in, I knew that the odds were in my favour.

Usually when I make my way through a forest, even when it's raining, I call as I advance. That day, however, the wind was whirring, causing such a ruckus that I was unable to manage any decent calls.

All of a sudden, I heard branches cracking somewhere to my right. I turned my head and spotted another moose just 10 m (32 ft.) away from me . . . and he was perfectly positioned to boot, although his head was slightly hidden behind a large fir. I took one step forward and saw a large point of his rack. Without hesitating, I shot my arrow and watched as it pierced the bull's body. Fatally injured, the bull took off, his immense rack brushing up against the alder trees as he fled, causing them to fall in his wake. The emotion and sheer beauty of the moment took my breath away.

We waited almost an hour before following the bull's tracks, giving him ample time to succumb to his injuries in peace. He hadn't gotten further than 100 m (328 ft.). He was a gorgeous specimen with a rack spanning 145 cm (57 in.) across. Sylvain and I were thrilled with our trophy. Obviously, without the rut pit camouflage we would never have been able to get as close to those moose as we did–the wind was just too loud and too strong that day. Rut pit mixture is the best scent cover-up you'll ever find, so next time you come across a wallow, jump right in and make the most of it!

A gorgeous specimen with a rack spanning 145 cm (57 in.) across, harvested in the Louise-Gosford controlled harvesting zone

HUNTING NEAR RUT PITS

1. SILENCE

If you don't use any calling techniques when hunting, you can stand watch near a fresh rut pit and get promising results nonetheless. A bull roams the area around his rut pits for several days. The best thing to do is position yourself approximately 30 m (100 ft.) from a wallow, in an area where you can easily move if need be. Generally, there will be several fresh rut pits in one area. If the thought of rolling around in a rut pit disgusts you, at least make sure to use the wind to your advantage.

2. CHARM

If you've mastered the art of calling, emitting a few female wails in close proximity to a rut pit can be well worth it. If your coveted bull is alone and not too far away, he won't hesitate to come looking for the female whose cries he just heard. However, if he's already accompanied by females, your calls might go unanswered as there's a pretty good chance he's already fully satisfied with his harem and isn't interested in going after yet another female. And remember, it's usually the female that goes looking for the group.

3. PROVOCATION

The first stage of provocation consists of imitating a male foraging the area: "Wrouahf, wrouahf." After a few calls, stop and listen for four or five minutes, then resume calling, slowly walking for another 50 or 75 m (165 or 246 ft.).

Next, rub your rattling pallet up against a few branches for 20 to 40 seconds, and start all over again.

When the owner of that rut pit gets wind of another male loitering around his territory, he'll quickly make his way back in a fit of jealousy, ready to confront the intruder.

The second stage consists of imitating a male in the presence of a female. Stroll around the wallow and alternate between a receptive female's wails and a male's response. This is sure to get your coveted bull all riled up.

"A fresh rut pit is
a clear indication that
a bull is in the vicinity."

CHAPTER 10

MATING SEASON: LOVE IS IN THE AIR

Moose are an interesting species to study and to hunt, and you need to adapt your technique to the time of year you plan on hunting them. However, regardless of whether you're hunting before, during or after rut season, one thing should never change: When you enter their territory, be and act just like them. That's exactly what I do, and it's an indispensable piece of advice. By acting and thinking like a moose, you're putting all the odds in your favour. Be patient and I'm convinced you'll experience some incredible hunting moments.

THE RUT CALENDAR

The three major hunting periods are before, during and after rut season, the times of which vary slightly across Canada. In most provinces, you can hunt moose from late August to early December, adapting your hunting techniques as the season progresses.

According to my observations and the opinion of several trusted biologists, rut dates are prone to regional variations. Most experts attribute these variations to temperature change or day length, technically known as the photoperiod, although the exact effect such factors have on moose seasonality is not clearly defined.

Generally speaking, rut season in Quebec tends to hit its peak between September 18th and October 5th, meaning that the majority of the province's calves are conceived during those three weeks (a period often referred to as "the big call"). Females who don't mate during this time will once again be in heat 23 or 24 days following the first ovulation (a period referred to as "the small rut").

I wish to stress the fact that my years of experience, both in the Yukon and Quebec, have led me to believe that these rut periods are the same from one area to the next and from year to year.

The peak of the rut is when the dominant bulls are at their most vulnerable. In contrast to the females and younger bulls, the dominant males progressively cease to eat, dedicating all their time to breeding. For approximately three weeks, every ounce of their energy is channelled into their reproductive drive. It's during this time that they dig their famous rut pits (see page 151).

Depending on where you're located, you might be hunting before, during or after the rut season. I've observed moose during all of these periods and studied the evolution of their behaviour throughout. Consequently, I always adapt my technique to the season when I'm hunting.

Put a group of hunting enthusiasts in the same room, and each one is bound to want to share, in great detail, why their technique is the best. However, it's important to understand that what works for one hunter, won't necessarily work for another, especially if said hunters don't hunt during the same period.

AUGUST

1	2	3	4	5	6	7
8	9	10	11	12	13	14
15	16	17	18	19	20	21
22	23	24	25	26	27	28
29	30	31				

SEPTEMBER

1	2	3	4	5	6	7
8	9	10	11	12	13	14
15	16	17	18	19	20	21
22	23	24	25	26	27	28
29	30					

OCTOBER

1	2	3	4	5	6	7
8	9	10	11	12	13	14
15	16	17	18	19	20	21
22	23	24	25	26	27	28
29	30	31				

NOVEMBER

1	2	3	4	5	6	7
8	9	10	11	12	13	14
15	16	17	18	19	20	21
22	23	24	25	26	27	28
29	30					

DECEMBER

1	2	3	4	5	6	7
8	9	10	11	12	13	14
15	16	17	18	19	20	21
22	23	24	25	26	27	28
29	30	31				

Production of rut pits
(September 7 - October 5)

Peak of rut season
(September 18 - October 5)

Small rut
(October 11 - October 28)

"When I enter moose territory, I become one of them and replicate their behaviour."

BEFORE THE RUT

Starting in late August and early September, the days begin to get considerably shorter, which causes a hormonal shift in moose. Females are just a few weeks from being in heat and males see their testosterone increase greatly. The result: Males begin to shed the velvet lining on their antlers and they begin to test their new weapons by rubbing them against trees and shrubs.

Usually at this time of year, the males are the only ones who are vocal. I've observed them daily and have come to understand their behaviour, realizing that they walk with a steady rhythm, emitting a loud "Wrouahf" here and there. This is the time of year when they begin to display themselves, letting others in proximity know that they're there. I've often witnessed impressive bulls move about in this way, walking 60 m (200 ft.) before stopping to listen. During this period in early September, males actively seek out other males, hoping to locate their whereabouts but keep their aggression in check. On more than one occasion, I've seen two males eating side by side, seemingly tolerating each other's presence. Once I even witnessed two males spend an entire week together.

I also noticed that in early September, both in Quebec and in the Yukon, males tend to gravitate towards mountaintops (while females prefer to stay close to lakes and other bodies of water). The fact that males seek out an area with strong winds is no coincidence. In fact, the strong winds allow males, whose antlers are shedding, to escape the mosquitoes that are attracted by the smell of the blood. Of course, the males leave the mountaintops from time to time in search of food and water, but they're not yet really interested in pursuing the females.

In my experience, in the weeks leading up to rut season, moose tend to follow a certain routine, and if they're not disturbed, they usually stay within the same general area until they run out of food and are forced to move on. During this period, the main concern for moose is their safety, which means they'd rather content themselves with plain old leaves, than go out in search of a decadent meal that might put their life at risk. Moose are far from being as gluttonous as bears or even deer; sure, they need to ingest an insane amount of food on a daily basis, but never at the expense of their own safety. It's therefore doubly important for a hunter to make as little suspicious noise as possible during this time. By suspicious noise I mean any sound that isn't a sound a bull would normally hear in his day-to-day activities. For example, if you decide to hunt in an area that hasn't been disturbed all summer long and you decide to start zipping around in your truck or all-terrain vehicle, there's a good chance the moose will change their habits and move on to a different sector. For much the same reason, I would suggest you don't set up camp on the edge of a potential hunting spot.

PRE-RUT
HUNTING TECHNIQUES

It's important to note that at this point in the season, females aren't very vocal. Males, on the other hand, are quite vocal, using their cries and antler rubbing as a means to warn other males of their presence. This is why, pre-rut, I stick entirely to male calls.

Armed with my rattling pallet, I practice Spot-and-Stalk hunting and keep an eye out for fresh signs of rubbing left behind by males. I slowly roam the area, producing a few "Wrouahfs" and lightly brushing my rattling pallet up against some branches.

I make sure to closely replicate a bull's behaviour, stopping for frequent pauses and listening for the presence of other males. I don't worry about the noise I make as I navigate the forest–a bull inevitably makes noise when he walks, so I make sure I do too. In my 40 years as a hunter, I have never seen a moose move branches out of the way before passing an obstacle, so why would I? Of course, I'm careful to not make noise with my bow or other hunting equipment, but any natural noise is fine.

When I see or hear a male, I make my way towards him, my demeanour unchanging. Males like to identify the other males who roam their territory, especially during this time of the year, so they'll have no issue with letting you get within shooting range just to be able to better assess you.

Be aware that, at the start of the season, it's always a little more difficult to visually locate a moose because the leaves haven't yet fallen from the trees, meaning the forest is still very dense. Because of this, it's even more important to determine where your coveted bull is, imitate his behaviour and listen attentively. Plus, because food is abundant, moose can basically eat wherever they want, which means they won't hesitate to change areas if they're the least bit disturbed.

DURING THE RUT

During rut season, dominant males court females using calls and by adopting a different behaviour: Their walk and posture changes and their physical contact increases. They lick their lips and, with their head bent low, they slowly approach the females. Females are usually scared of males and will ward them off, even going so far as to run away if the unwanted guests are overly aggressive. The only time a female is docile towards a male is when she's ready to mate.

Generally, females start ovulating around September 15th, although a small number might start a little earlier. It's also around this time that you're likely to come across fresh rut pits. Although I've witnessed a cow rolling around in a rut pit as early as September 15th, most rut-pit-related activities begin around the 20th. While it's true that photoperiod plays an important role on a female's ovulation, rut pits made by a dominant bull also have a considerable effect on this phenomenon.

Chances are you've met up with hunters hunting a few kilometres from your territory. And it's probably already happened that, in passing, you've discussed how your calls were successful and theirs weren't. Now, why is that?

First, I believe that the presence of one or more dominant males in a given area can have a huge influence on this. When dominant males make rut pits, they do so over a vast territory, which in turn, makes the females receptive more quickly. Add to that the fact that not all females are in heat at the same time and it's only natural that a female's receptivity will vary by a week, give or take, between two sectors.

The second explanation for why there can be such a difference between two territories is simple: One sector is devoid of moose. Most hunters are confined to small sectors and if the moose don't adopt your sector the week you're there, you can try all the strategies in the world, but it'll all be in vain.

Other factors, like the female-to-male ratio, should also be considered. The more balanced the ratio is, the more activity you're likely to witness. Don't forget: Moose are very jealous creatures and if they feel threatened by other suitors, they won't hesitate to confront them—even if there are enough females in the area to satisfy them both.

Combats
in the heart of the forest

It is during rut season that the big dominant males confront one another in order to establish who is the more dominant one, and thus, who will get all the females in that sector. During this period, the males have zero tolerance for one another–the females are in heat and it's an all-out war in the forest. I remember one male in particular who tolerated absolutely no other male on his territory. Imposing as he was, he had no trouble intimidating any intruder who came looking to seduce his females, even pursuing the intruders over long distances. Remember that moose are like humans– some are more aggressive, ready to fight at the drop of a hat, while others are more docile and avoid confrontation. When confronting your adversary, it's important to adapt to his character. It's typically around September 20th that you'll start to hear the season's first male skirmishes. Testosterone is at its peak and the slightest provocation is simply not tolerated. We hunters need to take advantage of this time. I've studied this phenomenon over the years and believe me when I say that the interactions between moose hit their peak between the last days of September and the first days of October. It is during this period that you'll hear the most interactions in the forest, and it's a magical thing to witness.

HUNTING TECHNIQUES DURING RUT SEASON

The most important thing during rut season is to locate the rut zone in your sector. In other words, you need to find those rut pits.

Remember that to provoke a male, you need to be in the right place at the right time. If you spend your time (and energy) calling in an area the moose don't visit during rut season, you're doing it all for nothing. However, if you've discovered a rut pit in a given sector, you can be sure that the chances of one or several males being in the area are very high. If the smell emanating from the pit isn't very strong, carefully survey your surroundings– you're likely to find a fresher one nearby.

Female calls yield little results pre-rut, but when breeding season officially kicks off, you need to start introducing them into your hunting routine. Personally, I like walking through the forest, imitating a moose couple. It's magical and the jealous males in the area can't resist. I move about imitating a female, then a male, all while rubbing my rattling pallet against the trees. I alternate between a female's protesting wails and a male's impatient grunts. I do my best to replicate the calls I normally hear in the forest. By doing so, if a male in the sector hears what he believes to be a rival bull with a female, he'll want to make himself known and

try to steal the female away. Don't hesitate to repeat the female's cries, making sure to vary their length and intensity. Varying is the key to success. A monotone cry might get you an answer, but you'll find it difficult to garner enough interest to attract your prey within shooting range. No two moose will react the same way to your calls and provocation techniques. Therefore, it's important that you always adapt to your adversary. It's normal for there to be lags when a bull is approaching you; don't rush things and stay confident.

When a bull starts making his way towards you in response to your calls or rattling, don't stay put–move around a little. If you stay in the same spot, your bull might decide to forgo the final few steps needed to get within shooting range. A few steps here or there (a few metres or a dozen or so feet) and a little branch snapping is enough to convince your adversary that you're indeed a rival bull.

Once again, it's important to replicate your adversary's behaviour. If your rival is still a good distance away, don't hesitate to meet him halfway–he'll just have less distance to travel before being close enough for you to shoot. If you're a hunter with reduced mobility and must remain stationary, this is still the period in which you'll have the most chances at getting a moose within shooting range. Just remember, to increase your chances of a harvest, you need to think like a moose. Moose like to move about, all while staying hidden as long as possible or remaining close to a hiding spot.

Close the distance that separates you from your prey according to your weapon. Spotting a moose 125 m (410 ft.) away is great, but if you hunt using a bow, you need to be within 85 m (280 ft.) of your target. Good luck! Of course, some moose are more daring than others and will come within 85 m of you, but many will turn around and run away instead. Be proactive and choose a territory that's slightly covered, one where the moose can wander about without feeling exposed or vulnerable.

BE PATIENT!

If I could offer you only one tip for rut season, it would be to be patient. Remember, moose are never in a hurry. They don't care if it takes five minutes or an entire hour to get to you. So be patient, persevere and adapt to their rhythm.

AFTER THE RUT

I find that calling techniques used after October 10th don't yield as many results and I don't generally recommend applying them to your post-rut hunting strategies. It's important to understand that more often than not, moose won't come to you after rut season . . . you have to go to them.

At this point in the season, bulls are coming out of a fast–they haven't eaten in a while–and winter is fast approaching. Therefore, their new main activity is eating to regain their strength and in preparation for the long months ahead. They need to store as much fat and energy as possible in order to survive the harsh cold they're about to endure.

Their testosterone levels have plummeted and their fierce competitive nature has subsided. The young males take advantage of this time to court the females that have not been claimed by the older bulls.

After rut season, moose limit their movements, choosing instead to remain in sectors where food is still available.

Males, accompanied by females and their calves, share what little fresh food they can still find.

After rut season, moose only occupy approximately 10% of their usual habitat, which is why you'll often see groups of moose in one area, fuelling up on food. And with the leaves having fallen from the trees, the forest is much less dense, making it easier for you to spot these groups from a distance.

Later in the season, look out for trees still adorned with fresh leaves. At this point in the year, moose tend to seek out birch and trembling aspen.

POST-RUT
HUNTING TECHNIQUES

As I mentioned before, after rut season a bull's testosterone levels drop considerably, and even though some males might still be seeking the few still-available females, calling is not the ideal technique to apply as of October 10th. Why is that? Well, your sector just might so happen to be devoid of any females, which means that all the males will have moved on to a different territory.

At this time of year, Stalk hunting is the only way to go. Personally, at this point in the season I imitate a male on the move, producing a "Wrouahf" from time to time and rubbing my rattling pallet against trees and shrubs along the way. I make sure my demeanour is calm and non-aggressive.

Males tolerate one another post-rut, so they won't feel threatened by you and will likely let you get close enough to shoot.

If you're an amateur hunter hunting from a platform or lookout tower, make sure to choose a sector that still has interesting food options for moose, otherwise the odds are against you.

Post-rut advantages

Calling after October 10th might not be the ideal tactic, but there are still some major advantages to the post-rut season:

• First off, because most of the leaves have fallen from the trees, you can spot moose more easily from a distance.

• Secondly, as I mentioned previously, moose tend to band together during this time, sharing what little food is still available.

• And finally, since you're more likely to hunt with a rifle at this time of year, you won't have to get as close to your target as when you hunt with a bow or crossbow.

CHAPTER 11

MEMORABLE
YUKON MOMENTS

Allow me to share some of my most unforgettable Yukon hunting moments with you. There's a reason why this immense territory is known as a moose (and hunter's!) paradise. In fact, some of my most impressive harvests took place in this majestic land. As a hunting guide, the Yukon has always been one of my destinations of choice.

MY FIRST YUKON HUNTING TRIP

With several harvests under my belt, a friend and I decided to watch a video entitled *Giants in the Yukon*. The moose starring in the video were huge! And I literally fell in love with the picturesque and pristine landscape–a veritable hunter's paradise.

I decided to contact the video's producer, who also happened to be a Yukon hunter, to see if he would allow me to hunt on his land. At the time, the cost of a hunting trip was $13,000. It was exorbitant, yes, but I absolutely wanted to live the experience. Dave Coleman, the owner of the outfitter establishment in question, assigned a guide to accompany me on my first Yukon excursion, (every non-resident is required to be accompanied by a guide).

My guide and I arrived together on the same plane, ready to hunt the giants that lurked around Earn Lake. That first Yukon expedition proved to be one of my most impressive: I harvested a large trophy male with a rack spanning 170 cm (67 in.). Imagine that! I recorded snippets of the trip with an old recorder of mine, and the images turned out to be pretty decent! Coming home from that hunting trip, I decided I would tour four villages to interview people as to whether they would be interested in attending hunting conferences. I showed everyone I met the images shot with my recorder and they were all blown away. I quickly realized that a conference on moose hunting in the Yukon would be a huge success. So, I headed back to the Yukon in preparation for another tour entitled *Yukon 2*. Not long after that trip, I visited more than 40 municipalities and "The Rack Man" was officially born.

2005: MY MOST MEMORABLE YEAR IN THE YUKON

Before recounting this wonderful story, I need to remind you of my trip to the Yukon the year before. In September 2004, Pierre Lamoureux, one of the hunters I was guiding for the first time, harvested a male with an antler span of 140 cm (55 in.) using a bow. Pierre was thrilled with his prize and continued to scout the land with me. My camera crew accompanied us everywhere we went, capturing the breathtaking landscape and majestic moose. One day, we spotted an enormous beast with an impressively large rack. I estimated his rack to be upwards of 178 cm (70 in.). I remember sitting in our boat, watching this incredible specimen wander the banks of Earn Lake. Pierre and I shared several looks, and I could tell that my partner was in complete awe of this enormous king. But seeing as we had already made our season's quota, we were unable to harvest our trophy male. What a shame!

That was the first time I spotted that moose around Earn Lake. What a beautiful, majestic, proud creature, roaming freely through the astounding Yukon landscape. I was already daydreaming about harvesting him during my next expedition. We captured the whole breathtaking scene on camera for my DVD *The Rack Man in the Yukon 3* and all the while I was thinking, "see you next year, buddy!"

The following year, during my 2005 Yukon hunting expedition, Pierre was once again by my side. The moment we reunited, we both had the same idea in mind–to find the trophy male from the year before. We spotted a few males and females in those first few days, but on the third day, we came across a majestic male with a rack that I estimated measured 165 cm (65 in.). He was accompanied by several females. Pierre, my cameraman Alexandre Domingue and I jumped in our boat and headed straight for that moose, calling as we approached. Suddenly, he stepped away from his harem and slowly began to make his way towards us.

To give you a better idea of the whole scene, I should point out that the piece of land separating us from the bull was an open clearing, sparse with regrowth and almost no density, therefore it was difficult to conceal our movements. When you're hunting with a bow under such conditions, it's extremely tough to get within shooting distance of your prey. And needless to say that when you're surrounded by a camera crew, the task is even more harrowing! Suddenly, I noticed that the male was getting a little suspicious. My two companions and I were trying desperately to move as one, but the open landscape was making

it extremely difficult. We just needed to walk another 6 or 7.5 m (19 or 24 ft.) for Pierre to be able to release his arrow. Our cameraman moved sideways for a better angle, suddenly causing the bull to high-tail it into the dense forest, never stopping to look back. What a disappointment! But that's hunting for you–you just never know what'll happen from one minute to the next. Pierre and I now had only one thing in mind–to find that monster male from the year before.

On the fourth day, as our boat slowly glided down the calm lake, I saw a rippling wave in the distance, near the shore. I squinted, then used my binoculars, but I couldn't see what caused the swell on the otherwise perfectly smooth surface. I veered the boat in the direction the wave came from, keeping my eyes peeled and my ears open.

Suddenly, a majestic creature appeared before me. He was putting on quite the spectacle, behaving in a way I had never seen a moose behave before. He was swinging his rack from left to right, but directly in the water. His submerged antlers were what caused the earlier wave. He began alternating smashing his antlers against the branches and swinging them back and forth in the water. This strange behaviour continued for quite some time, when suddenly he ceased his little angry ritual and looked me right in the eye. That's when I noticed how incredibly huge his rack was. Wow! What a beast!

We continued to make our way to shore, turning off the electric motor for the last hundred metres or so. I was struggling with the best way to proceed. Should I get off the boat and try to approach the moose with Pierre and my cameraman, at the risk of losing yet another trophy male? Or should our archer attempt to shoot the target from the boat with the engine at a complete stop, as required by hunting regulations?

I decided to go with the second option, which was also the safest. Now that you know me well, you know that shooting from a distance is not my preferred way of hunting–I much prefer the challenge of confronting my prey up close. But when you make a decision, you need to stand by it!

So there we were, nearing the bank. I was calling and the bull was answering, making his way directly towards us. Spotting a thicket near the shore, I directed the boat there and killed the motor. The moose was within shooting range, perfectly positioned. Pierre stretched his bow and released an arrow straight into the animal's kill zone. The bull arched his back, charged towards the water and suddenly stopped in his tracks.

Pierre Lamoureux's trophy rack measures 183 cm (72 in.) across.

He inhaled deeply, Pierre's arrow firmly in place. He stumbled a bit, slowly making his way towards the lake, and less than three minutes after the arrow penetrated his vital organs, he fell over.

He was an enormous bull with a rack spanning 183 cm (72 in.). After weighing all his parts, he totalled an impressive 748 kg (1649 lbs.) pre-kill. Upon further inspection, we happily realized we had just harvested the huge beast from the year before.

And then there were two!

The second hunter I accompanied that season was Jean-Marie Veilleux. He too wanted to harvest a moose using a bow, but approaching the males proved to be quite the challenge during the trip. Finally, two days before the end of our expedition, we spotted a large male with a rack measuring 166 cm (65 ½ in.)–a spectacular beast! He was even larger than Pierre's moose, easily weighing 50 kg (110 lbs.) more, for a total of 800 kg (1764 lbs.). To this day, that bull is still the biggest moose harvested during one of my Yukon hunting trips.

That same year, again during one of my Yukon stays, I had the chance to get within just a few metres of a mature bull, thanks to my famous imitating, rattling and calling techniques.

The result? I shot that male with my bow and arrow from just 4.5 m (15 ft.) away! An impressive rack spanning 152 cm (60 in.) . . . what more could I ask for?

And finally, Denis Beauchamp was also successful that year, harvesting an impressive male on the third day of our trip. I'll never forget it: Denis had spotted a male with a huge rack on our very first day and he absolutely wanted to shoot him right then and there. For him, that moose was the trophy of a lifetime.

I stopped him from shooting by placing my hand over his gun's barrel! I think that he's since forgiven me, seeing as two days later he harvested a beautiful trophy with a rack spanning 165 cm (65 in.) across!

An exceptional hunting season

That year proved to be an exceptional hunting year. Four impressive trophies with rack spans of 152, 165, 166 and 183 cm (60, 65, 65 ½ and 72 in.) respectively! I remember wrapping up filming for my DVD with a shot of me proudly standing behind those remarkable racks, MacMillan River Outfitters camp in the background. An unforgettable trip and certainly one of my most memorable to date! We went looking for those famous Earn Lake giants and find them we most certainly did!

THE HUNT
OF A LIFETIME

The Yukon is, without a doubt, a true hunter's paradise–a vast landscape abounding with game where you'll be blown away by the breathtaking scenery at every turn, every mountain you spot in the distance, every glistening lake you come across . . . and every single hunting expedition you take.

Despite all my success as a hunter thus far, I still harboured a dream: To harvest a beast of a moose, one that would earn me a world record in the bow-hunting category.

From the very first time I stepped foot in the Yukon, I did everything I could to make that dream come true, but as you and I know, when it comes to hunting, nothing is guaranteed. I mean think about it–a hunter from Quebec being awarded with a Pope and Young world record! Impossible? Oh no, my friend!

My dream came true on September 18, 2008, a date that is forever engraved in my mind. Come to think of it, I probably should have bought myself a lottery ticket that day!

A client of mine, Steven Simard from Rivière-du-Loup, was accompanying me on that trip. Steven had landed himself a trophy male just a few days prior, one with an impressive 139-cm (55-in.) rack. I still had a few days before my next client was due to arrive and, being the hunting guide that I am, I'm sure you have no problem believing the fact that I don't often take time off! I prefer to spend as much time as possible in the forest.

So on that day, Steven and I headed out; I was armed with my bow and Steven with his camera, meaning I had two cameramen to help film my excursion. We were navigating down a lake, when after some time, I spotted one female, then a second with her calf. Even though we were navigating at high speed, two enormous white masses about 125 m (410 ft.) behind the females and calf caught my attention. Those masses had me a little perplexed;

I had never seen them before, despite having scouted that entire area hundreds of times before. The masses weren't moving, so I figured they weren't antlers, but I just had to be absolutely sure.

I decided to turn off the motor and take advantage of the windless day to make a few non-receptive female calls. Grabbing my binoculars, I returned my attention to the white masses in the distance and, to my surprise, saw that they began to move. The bull, who was lying down, suddenly stood up in response to my calls. Just the sign I needed to pursue this mysterious moose. I knew he was impressively large, but I had to discover just how large.

I steered the boat closer to shore, making sure to keep my distance from the females. Followed by my two cameramen, I walked for about 20 minutes, getting as close to the bull as possible. I crossed the 450 m (492 yards) that separated me from him, continuously calling out in imitation of a male getting ready to confront another. With every rattling sound I made with my pallet, the bull was getting more and more aggressive. We were walking towards one another and confrontation was now inevitable.

It was only when I got within 60 m (200 ft.) of my adversary that I realized just how imposing in stature he was. In fact, I had never before seen such a striking male. Was a world record bull standing right before my very eyes? The bull was so impressive in size that adrenaline was coursing through my body, reminding me of my very first harvest. Sure, I had encountered many a moose in my life, and I had learned long ago how to control my emotions, but this was a magical moment–the moment I had dreamed about my whole life! I felt confident, and yet my heart was beating a thousand miles a minute; I knew that the task at hand was going to be a challenging one, especially with two cameramen following my every move, enamoured by this once-in-a-lifetime experience. To be honest, I was terrified that one of my companions would make that one false move that would cost me the harvest of a lifetime.

Turning to look at them, I motioned for them to stop moving. Both were positioned at different angles, ready to capture the moment on camera. It was imperative that they execute the task at hand while remaining completely still. All I had left to do was convince the monstrous bull to come within shooting–and filming–range. I needed to be 100% sure of my shot before releasing my arrow.

As luck would have it, the bull continued to make his way towards me. When he was about 30 m (100 ft. give or take) from me, he started to parade about, swinging his head back and forth, trying to intimidate me out of a confrontation. However, instead of showing his girth by zigzagging from left to right, he was approaching me head-on, making it impossible for me to release an arrow into his kill zone. The 10 ½-year-old male hadn't become the king of the forest for nothing, and despite my proximity, the battle was still far from won.

Aside from 2.5 m (8 ft.) of regrowth, the only thing separating me from my adversary was a single tree. The bull was still facing me, less than 9 m (30 ft.) away. Not knowing in what direction he was going to go next, I decided to draw my bow in the hopes I would get the chance to shoot. I was acutely aware of the fact that I could no longer lower my bow as the slightest movement would send my adversary running in the opposite direction.

One minute ticked by, then two. The bull was standing completely still and my bow was getting harder and harder to hold. The suspense was palpable. My arms were beginning to falter and I knew I wouldn't be able to hold out much longer. Thankfully my adrenaline was pumping, and knowing I would probably never get another opportunity like this again, I managed to hold on just a little longer.

All of a sudden, the bull resumed walking in my direction. This wasn't what I wanted, as I still didn't have a clear shot. And even if I could have shot my arrow, I ran the risk of the bull charging towards me, thus putting my cameraman in danger. Lucky for me, my adversary suddenly decided to step around the tree separating us from one another. Only 2.5 m (8 ft.) now stood between me and my 707-kg (1559-lbs.) trophy male. Being so close to such a towering bull is like coming face-to-face with a mammoth! In that split second, my adversary made a decision he wouldn't have time to regret. Turning to his side, he continued to advance, but this time, his flank was fully exposed. Just a few more steps . . . and bam! I released my arrow.

Because of the short distance that separated us (and because it didn't have time to stabilize in the air), the arrow penetrated the animal only halfway. The moose took off, straight ahead, following a path that made it easy for my cameraman to catch the whole scene on film.

The unthinkable had just occurred: I had harvested a record-breaking bull. I was filled with emotion. My hands were shaking, the tremor in my voice and the tears in my eyes a clear indication of the intense happiness I was feeling. And then, all of a sudden, all I could think was, "Did my cameraman catch this once-in-a-lifetime moment?" Today I know they did, but believe me when I say it wasn't until I saw the footage with my own two eyes that I could rest easy!

After waiting an hour (an hour that seemed to last a lifetime!), we set off in search of my trophy. When I finally found him, my emotions hit an all-time high. I flung my fists up in the air, victorious! Today I can finally say that it's official: I, Réal Langlois, Rack Man and small-towner, hold the world record for the largest moose harvested with a bow. Weighing in at 707 kg (1559 lbs.) with a massive rack spanning 193 cm (76 in.) across and 27 points, my trophy male was the biggest to be hunted in the Yukon in 2008.

201

"My world record:
A 707-kg (1559-lbs.) bull
with a 193-cm (76-in.) rack
adorned with 27 points."

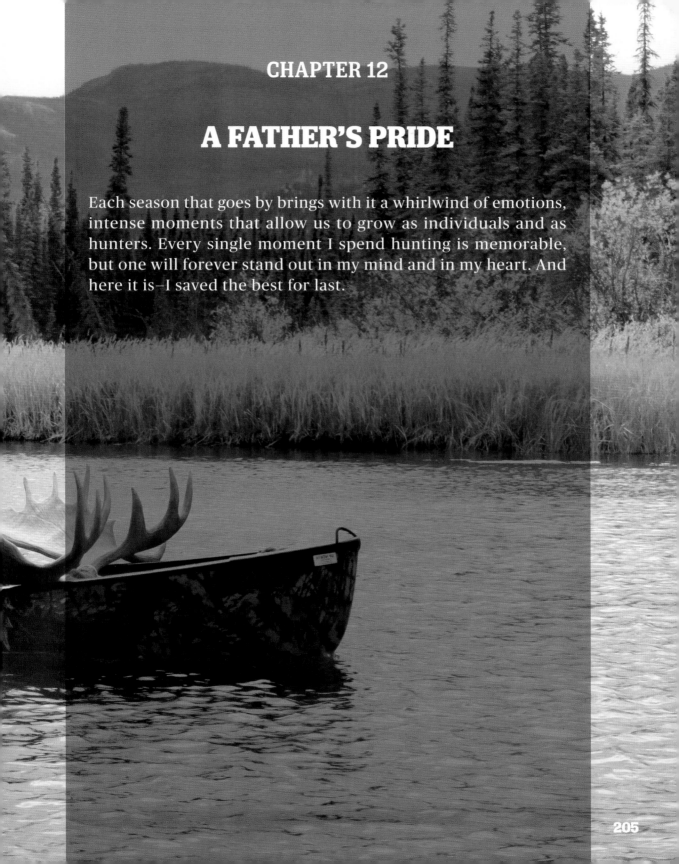

CHAPTER 12

A FATHER'S PRIDE

Each season that goes by brings with it a whirlwind of emotions, intense moments that allow us to grow as individuals and as hunters. Every single moment I spend hunting is memorable, but one will forever stand out in my mind and in my heart. And here it is–I saved the best for last.

THE AWAKENING OF EARN LAKE

On September 11, 2009, Kevin, my son and best friend, arrived in the Yukon. Finally prying himself away from his computer screens and editing studio, Kevin had the opportunity to see Earn Lake for the first time. I took advantage of the occasion to show him in person the places where some of my earliest best memories were made.

During the next two days, temperatures dropped, causing the moose to move around quite a bit. Now was my chance to show Kevin some of my hunting techniques. As I began sharing, I couldn't help but wonder if he was actually listening to a word I was saying, or if he was completely hypnotized by the beauty that surrounded him. We were lucky enough to see a few imposing males, and proving once again the efficacy of my techniques, we even managed to get close to them. In all, we spotted five males and one female, but none were particularly impressive in size. I like to think back on that day as the "awakening of Earn Lake."

One of our encounters was exceptionally memorable. We came within 5 m (16 ft.) of a beautiful bull moose. My son was a little nervous, accustomed as he was to seeing these impressive creatures on computer screens in his editing room, not up close and in person! His first live experience had him looking back at me and exclaiming, "the rest of our hunting trip is looking promising!"

It was the morning of September 14, 2009. Superstar, the notorious bull that wanted to run me out of the woods just a few days prior, was back, parading around like he was putting on a private show. I'll never forget it. That moose proved to me that I could still be surprised by these creatures' behaviour. For over 40 minutes, Superstar confronted me. He could hear me talking to Kevin about vocalizations and rattling, and he still just stood there! Several times, he started to approach me, but I think he understood that I was the dominant male. What an incredible thing to witness!

"See, Kevin, this is the most important hunting lesson I could teach you. When you see a bull like him, here's what you have to do. First, you need to call out with a 'Wrouahf, wrouahf.' Then, as soon as he spots you, raise your antlers. He won't thoroughly examine you to see if you are indeed a moose–in his mind, he's dealing with another male. So in situations like this, Kevin, you do as I do: You slowly advance, you stop, you start again, follow the bull's rhythm. Follow me."

"This is cool . . ."

"No, this is *really* cool. And now look, we advanced several times and I've been playing with him for over 40 minutes."

"He won't stop scratching the ground."

"Do you know why he's doing that?"

"No."

"It's his way of telling the other male, 'this is MY territory.' Soon, he's going to urinate."

"Yeah."

"Look, he's doing it again. This is the greatest hunting lesson you could have witnessed. You know, everyone likes to share their hunting techniques. But the best technique? Just do what the moose does. It's as simple as that. I didn't come up with some elaborate schema–I just watch and learn. It's nothing new, you understand? I just imitate what the moose do. See how easy it is?

"Yeah."

"You advance, you stop and you look at him. He'll do some rattling, so you do some rattling in return. Eventually, you'll meet halfway."

A little later that same day, sitting comfortably by Earn Lake, we spotted some moose through our binoculars. I turned to my son and said: "On top of that big mountain over there, I always see mature males. Not every single day, but every year I spot some."

All of a sudden, I spotted yet another moose.

"I see one on the tip of that point to our left. Look–it's an impressive male."

"Yes, I see it too."

"Come, we'll head over there by boat. That's an imposing bull, just like I like them!"

Without losing another second, we folded up our camping chairs, jumped in our boat and headed towards the point where the moose was, taking a longer detour so as not to frighten him. As we neared our destination, we relied on the boat's electric motor to get us to shore, while trying to make as little noise as possible. As we stepped off the boat, I turned to Kevin to give him some last-minute advice.

"Follow in my footsteps like you were doing this morning. Do exactly as I do."

I slowly began to make my way towards our trophy, calling and rattling as I went. The moose turned and entered the forest, giving me the perfect opportunity to up my pace and approach him without being seen. We could hear him rustling about in the branches. I continued to make my way towards him, rubbing my rattling pallet against the trees and listening to the sounds coming from his direction. The stunning male was regularly calling out at this point, and I was answering him each time without fail, just as I've always taught my fellow hunters to do. Our dialogue was under way.

I could see the moose; he wasn't very far away. He was slowly moving about, swinging his rack from left to right in an attempt to show me he was in combat mode. I told Kevin to immediately move to my left and get his bow ready. The male was still slowly moving, parallel to where we stood, but with not enough room for a clear shot.

Kevin was poised and ready and the bull was slowly moving towards a small clearing, his entire kill zone clearly visible and unobstructed. Kevin released his arrow and it hit the moose, causing him to run off in the direction of the lake where he suddenly stopped moving. He was fatally injured and Kevin knew it. I invited my son to make his way towards the lake, ready to release a second arrow in order to stop his prey from advancing

any further into the water. Kevin shot a second time, his arrow hitting its target with precision, and the great creature kneeled over almost instantly, just 60 m (200 ft.) from where we stood. Ecstatic, I reached out to congratulate my son.

"Yessssss! A dream come true, harvesting a moose with my son!"

Kevin and I both had tears in our eyes, overcome with emotion. It was such a perfect experience: Our third day of hunting, the approach, the shot, a stunning male with an impressive rack, Kevin's first kill . . . and with a bow to boot! The bull's rack spanned 142 cm (56 in.) across and was magnificent.

I felt exactly as I had the previous year when I shot my record-breaking moose. But this time, it was my son's moose. What a great gift from the universe, one of the most amazing memories to create with your offspring! I can scream it from the rooftops now–I was so proud of my son that day!

Ten years earlier, I had shared the story of my first Yukon expedition with Kevin, and now I was experiencing it with him– no words could express what I was feeling. To parents whose children are passionate about hunting, I urge you to share their passion and introduce them to hunting as early as possible. They'll be forever grateful, of that I am sure.

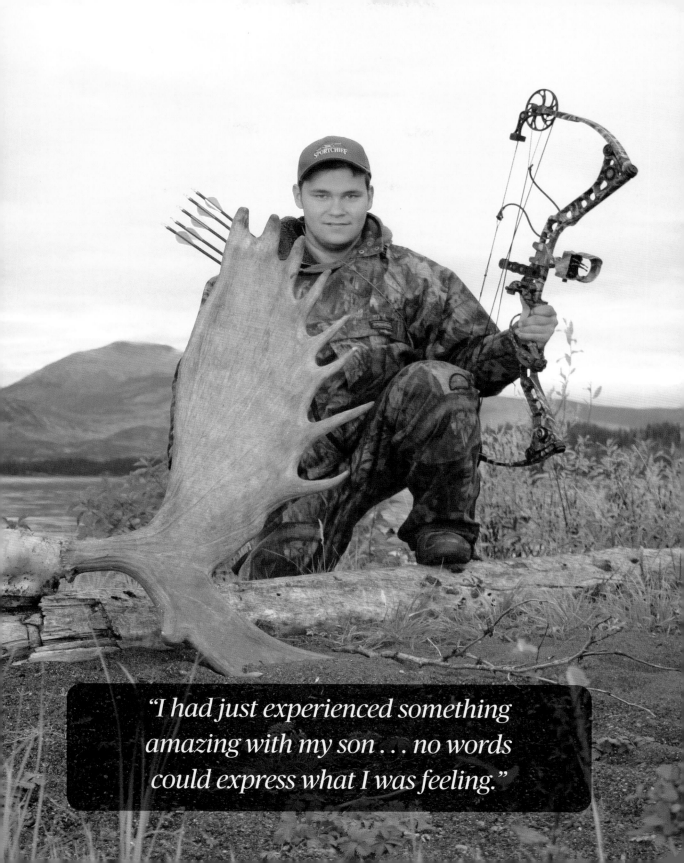

"I had just experienced something amazing with my son . . . no words could express what I was feeling."

CONCLUSION

In conclusion, I'd like to reiterate that no hunting technique is 100% infallible. No two moose will ever react the same way. The main thing to remember is to hunt in a territory you know has moose, consider the weather, camouflage your natural scent, attract moose to you, act like a moose and accept the fact that a moose won't always react the way you think he should!

If I one day stumble upon a magic lamp from which a genie emerges telling me he'll grant me three wishes I think I'll have to tell him that my three wishes have already come true; my first wish was to set a world record in bow-hunting, which I did in 2008; my second wish was to harvest a moose with my son Kevin, which happened in 2009; and my third wish came true in 2010 when, at almost 50 years old, I received the most beautiful testimony of my hunting career. During one of my conferences, I asked the audience who among them was the youngest hunter to harvest a moose. A young man of 14 raised his hand. I asked him to join me onstage. The young man then proceeded to tell the entire room how the previous year he had harvested a male with a 137-cm (54-in.) rack using a bow and arrow. I asked him to explain in detail how he managed such an impressive feat.

"I was in my watchtower, calling out. I heard a female and a mature male answer back. I was extremely nervous, but I kept calling regardless. The bull kept answering but refused to come my way. That's when I remembered the advice you shared with me the year before, Mr. Langlois. You said that when a situation such as this one occurs, hunters need to approach the moose, not wait for the moose to approach them.

"So, I climbed down from my watchtower and started to move in the direction the bull's calls were coming from. As I neared, I hid in a small clearing and used your pallet to do a little rattling. That garnered a few responses and the male eventually started to make his way towards me. But then the female called out and the male turned back towards her. Therefore, I did some more rattling, hoping to turn his attention back to me. And it worked, except then the female started to wail and the male left in search of her. I called out again. I could hear him coming towards me but I couldn't see him. I was beginning to get a little discouraged. I didn't know what to do next and I even thought of giving up. But then I thought of you, Mr. Langlois, and how in your DVDs and during your conferences you say to never give up, that in situations like this one, it's important to continue approaching your adversary.

"So I started to make my way towards that bull, rattling as I went along. When he was about 12 m (40 ft.) from me, I readied my bow, released my arrow and killed my very first moose. I never would have succeeded if it weren't for your indispensable advice. I harvested that moose thanks to you, Mr. Langlois."

The entire room erupted in applause and, to be honest, the story even brought tears to my eyes.

Dear friends and readers, I, Réal Langlois aka The Rack Man, sincerely hope that this book will be the key to harvesting the trophy moose you've been longing for.

ABOUT THE AUTHOR

Réal Langlois was born in 1960 in Magog, Quebec. In 1976, he travelled to Abitibi-Témiscamingue with his father for his very first hunting expedition, where he harvested his first bull. From that moment on, his passion for hunting never waned.

Season after season, for over 40 years now, Réal has fuelled his passion for hunting, travelling across Canada and perfecting the art of bow and rifle hunting. He spends countless hours studying the behaviour of moose in a variety of territories and developing calling techniques and innovative Stalk hunting techniques, both of which have garnered him unrivalled success wherever he goes.

In the early 2000s, he travelled to the picturesque Yukon, deep in the heart of the wild, where the "giants" of the forest were believed to be. The first moose he harvested there was an impressive bull with a rack spanning 170 cm (67 in.) across. The whole experience was caught on camera.

That was the start of an amazing Yukon experience. Ever since that first trip, Réal has been undertaking yearly trips to the Yukon as a guide and film producer.

In September 2008, one of Réal's biggest dreams came true when he harvested a monster bull of 707 kg (1559 lbs.) with a rack span of 193 cm (76 in.).

This incredible trophy, harvested from only 2.5 m (8 ft.) away, earned Réal a Pope and Young record-breaking 249 points, forever changing the life of the man we've come to know as The Rack Man.

Réal is the popular host of conferences all across Quebec. He is also a hunting instructor, TV show host for channels CIMT, CHAU, CFTF, Wild TV and the Sportsman Channel (United States) and a regular contributor to the magazine *Sentier Chasse-Pêche*. Rack Man products and DVDs are sold in several specialty boutiques across Canada and the United States.

ACKNOWLEDGEMENTS

I would like to thank Modus Vivendi Publishing for giving me the opportunity to publish my book, both in French and in English. Thank you to my publisher, Marc Alain, and to my editorial director, Isabelle Jodoin. A very special thank you to my content editor, Nolwenn Gouezel, who helped me transform my manuscript into a book, and to Philip Church for his good advice on the English edition. Thank you to Émilie Houle, who did an amazing job on the design of this book.

I would also like to take a moment to thank my father, Joseph-Aimé, who introduced me to hunting. It's the most precious gift he could have given me. It has allowed me to earn an honourable living. Thanks, Dad!

Thank you to Patrice Mercier who helped me harvest my very first moose and gave me indispensable advice on moose calling. Thank you to the legendary Monsieur Orignal, Pierre Guilbault, who helped me practice my vocalizations in my early hunting days.

For several years now, my son Kevin has also been my partner, confidant and video editor. Two years ago, my other son, Simon, joined our team as a cameraman and video editor. Their contribution is my greatest reward to date.

I'd like to give a special mention to *Aventure Chasse et Pêche* which was, under the leadership of Denis Lapointe, the first magazine to give me a chance and publish several of my texts on moose hunting.

Thank you to Yves Laroche, columnist for the magazine *Sentier Chasse-Pêche*, for helping me write some of my pieces.

A heartfelt thank you to the two individuals who wrote my preface: Yves Laroche and Stéphan Lebeau.

Thank you to Christian Dussault, biologist and researcher for the Ministère des Ressources naturelles et de la Faune du Québec, for providing me with several moose studies.

A special thank you to the administrative team and members at the Louise-Gosford controlled harvesting zone in Lac-Mégantic, who allowed me to study the behaviour and customs of moose on their territory for years. Thank you also to MacMillan River Adventures in the Yukon for their incredible support in my quest to harvest my trophy moose. Thank you to all the cameramen, cooks, collaborators, as well as all my sponsors (thank you to Sportchief's Philippe Hardy for his undying loyalty and support). I'd also like to thank the Simard family in Rivière-du-Loup (owners of CIMT, CHAU and CFTF) for broadcasting my TV show for the past decade.

Finally, I'd like to thank you, my fellow hunters, for coming to my conferences, for watching my DVDs and for allowing me to share my passion with you. I hope this book brings you one step closer to harvesting the trophy moose of your dreams!

Réal Langlois aka The Rack Man

THE RACK MAN'S TOP PICKS

- Excalibur: Top-quality crossbows, made in Canada
  www.excaliburcrossbow.com

- Mathews Solocam: Bows
  http ://mathewsinc.com

- Browning: Firearms
  www.browning.com

- Sportchief: Hunting gear and apparel
  www.sportchief.com

REFERENCES

PROVINCIAL WILDLIFE MINISTRIES

Alberta
www.aep.alberta.ca

British Columbia
www.for.gov.bc.ca/mof/offices.htm

Manitoba
www.gov.mb.ca/conservation/wildlife/hunting

New Brunswick
www2.gnb.ca

Newfoundland and Labrador
www.env.gov.nl.ca

Nova Scotia
www.novascotia.ca/natr

Ontario
www.ontario.ca/hunting

Prince Edward Island
www.gov.pe.ca/forestry/wildPEI

Quebec
www.mffp.gouv.qc.ca/faune/chasse/index.jsp

Saskatchewan
www.saskatchewan.ca/environment

TERRITORIES' WILDLIFE MINISTRIES

Northwest Territories
www.enr.gov.nt.ca

Nunavut
www.gov.nu.ca/environment

Yukon Territory
www.env.gov.yk.ca

PHOTO CREDITS